Effective
Marketing

Geoffrey Randall

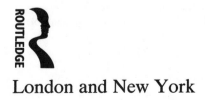

London and New York

First published 1994
by Routledge
11 New Fetter Lane, London EC4P 4EE

Simultaneously published in the USA and Canada
by Routledge
29 West 35th Street, New York, NY 10001

© 1994 Geoffrey Randall

Typeset in Times by Solidus (Bristol) Limited
Printed and bound in Great Britain by
Biddles Ltd, Guildford and King's Lynn

British Library Cataloguing in Publication Data

A catalogue reference for this book is available from the British Library.

Library of Congress Cataloging in Publication Data

Randall, Geoffrey.
    Effective marketing/Geoffrey Randall.
    p. cm. – (Self development for managers series)
    Includes bibliographical references and index.
    1. Marketing.   I. Title.   II. Series: Self development for
    managers.
    HF5415.R322   1994
    658.8–dc20   94–2995
                                                                        CIP

ISBN 0–415–10236–7

— *Contents*

List of figures   vi
Series editor's preface   vii

1 What is marketing about?
    What it can and cannot do   1
2 Understanding what we can't control
    Environments, markets, competitors   17
3 Understanding customers and consumers
    The most important people in our world   31
4 Information for marketing
    What do we need to know and how do we find out? 45
5 Using what we can control
    The marketing mix, segmentation and targeting 59
6 Existing products, new products
    Deciding what we should be offering our customers 73
7 Setting the price
    Satisfying marketing and profit objectives 91
8 Communicating with markets
    What do we want to communicate, to whom and how? 105
9 Distributing the products
    Getting our products to the right place at the right time 121
10 Putting it all together
    Strategy and planning 131

References   149
Index   151

— *Figures*

1.1 Marketing and the concept of matching 4
1.2 Marketing organisation 8
1.3 The product–service spectrum 12
2.1 The product life cycle 24
2.2 What happens in the different stages of the product
life cycle 25
4.1 Information and decision making 47
10.1 Porter's generic strategies 133
10.2 Ansoff's matrix 134

Series editor's preface

Most managers in the 1990s need to be able to work cross-functionally. In order to do this effectively an understanding of the main functional areas of management is a prerequisite. The Self-development for Managers Series is being developed to enable managers to contribute in each of the areas.

There is often a lack of understanding of the role and importance of marketing. In some organisations, particularly service organisations, everyone assumes responsibility for marketing. Everyone in turn serves a customer, internal to the organisation or external as the organisation strives to provide total quality service.

Effective Marketing, like other books in the series, has been written in a step-by-step approach designed to enable managers to apply the tools, techniques and frameworks to their own work situation. Managers are most likely to benefit by completing the activities at the end of each chapter. Once managers have read this book they may be interested in others which address functional areas such as *Accounting for Managers, The Self-reliant Manager,* which takes a strategic perspective on human resource issues, and *Step-by-Step Competitive Strategy,* which helps managers contribute more effectively to the future strategic direction of their business.

Geoffrey Randall was carefully chosen to write this book as a teacher of marketing, an author and a consultant with practical marketing experience. Helped by this blend of experience, Geoffrey has been able to give readers a good understanding of the marketing function and motivate them to apply their new knowledge and skills to their own work situation.

Jane Cranwell-Ward
Series Editor

1 *What is marketing about?*

What it can and cannot do

Marketing is one of the best-known and least understood words in the business language. We are all consumers, we are all bombarded every day with advertising messages and product offerings, many of us make buying decisions at work. Yet few people understand what marketing is really about. More seriously, there are many misconceptions of what it is, and what marketing managers do.

Consider the way the term is popularly used. Phrases such as, 'a marketing ploy' or 'the marketing people have obviously got hold of this', suggest that marketing is essentially manipulative: a way of tricking buyers, or putting a slant on reality which misrepresents the underlying truth.

An allied view is that marketing can somehow persuade us to buy things we do not really want or need. Again, the assumption is that the clever marketing people can deceive and manipulate us. A little thought will show that this view is both patronising and flattering: patronising because it is always other people who are being fooled by these tactics, not ourselves; and flattering because it accords marketing enormous power over our decisions, a power which marketing managers would doubtless like to have, but which is in fact illusory.

When did you last buy something merely because of a marketing ploy? When were you last persuaded to buy something you did not really need by clever advertising? The answer may be, 'Well, I did once', or 'A long time ago'; most of the time we buy what will meet our needs, will solve a particular problem, will give us particular satisfaction. We have a choice between competing products and brands, and if we make a less than satisfactory choice once, usually we do not repeat it.

■ Therefore, marketing is first of all about providing products which people want or need.

It is worth spending a little time on this idea of wants and needs, as some people try to distinguish between them. Critics of advertising and marketing in particular sometimes try to suggest that there are 'needs' which are good, and 'wants' which are somehow rather disreputable (and what those nasty marketing people are trying to foist on you). In fact, basic needs are really rather few: food and water, shelter, sex, family, society. For most members of advanced societies today, these basic needs are met most of the time. Beyond that, we are all exercising choice: which type and brand of food to buy, what sort of transport to use, which clothes to wear, how to entertain ourselves.

This is the domain in which marketing comes into play.

■ Companies survive and prosper by being better than competitors at providing what people want or need.

Again think of your own buying decisions, whether in your business or private life. You buy what best meets your needs out of the competing products available. The reasons for your preference may be based on price ('These are the cheapest paper clips' or 'This is the most expensive watch you can buy'); or on quality ('This machine – or this bank – will provide the benefits I want and will provide a high level of service'); or on personal preference ('I prefer this hairdresser to the others' or 'This brand suits my personal image – or the company's – better').

Chapter 3 will look in more detail at organisational and consumer buying behaviour. We should just note here that it is not enough simply to distinguish between consumer buying, which is somehow 'irrational', and industrial or organisational buying which is 'rational'. In the different buying situations we all find ourselves in, we have differing levels of expertise; but the person buying for a household is probably just as expert in the various fields covered by the family's needs as the purchasing manager in those covered by the company's. All buying decisions involve a variety of influencing factors, some capable of objective measurement, and others more subjective; this is true of company decisions just as much as of consumers.

Finally, in this preliminary exploration of what marketing is about, we must add the third element: the company itself. It is obviously naive to say simply that a company should provide what the market wants better than competitors, regardless of the costs. The company has to stay in business, and to do that it has to make a profit (the application of marketing ideas to other organisations is returned to later in this chapter). Not all companies can meet all needs; not all companies have the same resources or skills; not all companies are run by the same sort of people for the same sort of reasons. Each company will have objectives and constraints, and marketing will both contribute to the definition of those and work within them.

■ Therefore, our evolving definition of marketing must bring in this idea of *matching*:
■ Matching what the company is and wants to be, with what the market wants
■ Taking account of competitors' likely actions

This idea of what marketing is about is summed up in Figure 1.1, and will be referred to throughout the book. This is a definition of the broad marketing concept, and we now need to go on and examine what that means as a function within the business.

MARKETING AS A BUSINESS FUNCTION

The broad idea of marketing outlined above can lead to the view that 'Marketing is everything, and everything is marketing.' After all, if a business does not continue to meet the needs of the marketplace at a profit, it will die; but that is not a lot of help in deciding what marketing actually does in a particular firm. In some fields, it is possible to say that 'Everyone in the company is the marketing department', especially in service companies; everyone in the company contributes to the final delivery of a quality service. This is a useful idea, particularly when allied to a total quality approach; it can be valuable in breaking down departmental barriers which grow up in many firms and which actually work against meeting customer needs; but it is difficult to apply to every department in every firm, especially large ones.

What marketing should do is to contribute its view of where markets are going to the general debate about the company's

Figure 1.1 Marketing and the concept of matching

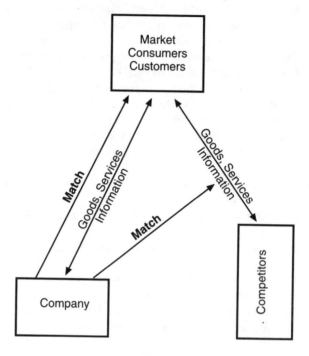

objectives and strategy. Each company will have its own history, its own assets, its own values and style. It is not appropriate for marketing to say, like the countryman giving directions, 'If I was you, I wouldn't start from here.' Equally, marketing must say, 'The needs of the market are changing in the following ways, and we must change to keep ahead or abreast of competitors.'   The message given by marketing is often seen by the rest of the firm as challenging or unwelcome, simply because it is marketing's job to track what is happening outside the firm, and try to ensure that the firm adapts. Change is always difficult, and doing what we have done for years is comfortable. But markets change, and competitors move on; marketing as a function must lead the company in considering market needs as well as other considerations such as shareholder demands, financial targets, productive use of assets and the needs of the workforce.

■ At this corporate level, therefore, marketing's role is to make sure that the customer and consumer are the focus of the business.

(The term customer is used in this book to mean an organisation buying for its own use or for re-sale, while consumer refers to the final buyer at the retail level, i.e. all of us in our private capacity.)

This seems simple and logical enough, and indeed many companies would say that they subscribe to it. These days, many firms have mission statements and slogans which commit them to 'meeting customer needs' or 'delivering the highest quality service to our customers'. Unfortunately, as we all know to our cost, not all firms consistently deliver on this commitment. We will return to this problem later in this chapter, since it is crucial to what marketing can and should contribute to the firm's performance.

At this stage, let us just note that how much influence the marketing function has in a company varies enormously. It is usually seen at its greatest in large firms making fast-moving consumer goods (known as FMCG: the brands advertised on television and stocked in supermarkets and chain stores). It may also be great in small, entrepreneurial, firms which have to be responsive to market needs to survive. It is often at its least influential in heavy engineering or high-technology companies. Within these broad generalisations, each company within an industry may vary, and different firms will vary over time. Much depends on the top managers in place at a particular time. The organisational reality is that personalities, politics and power do matter. The ideas put forward by marketing may be 'right', but to be accepted and acted on they also need to fit the company and its circumstances.

■ A central problem for marketing will always be the potential conflict between its overarching claim to strategic direction and its probably less powerful position politically.

The marketing function must therefore argue its case with other departments, and demonstrate that it has something unique to offer. What that is has been suggested by the broad concept defined earlier. In practice, we can say that

■ Marketing contributes to the definition and delivery of sustainable competitive advantage and that its unique contribution is

■ To define customer/consumer needs
■ To identify a positioning for the company's products and services
  which is different from competitors'
■ To communicate to customers and consumers the existence and
  unique benefits of the products
■ And to ensure that the products are available when and where they
  are needed

Exactly how this is done is the subject of this book. Before moving
into the detail, we will look at some organisational issues, at some
problems of implementing marketing, and at the different contexts
in which marketing may apply.

HOW SHOULD MARKETING BE ORGANISED?

It follows from the comments above that marketing departments
vary in their size, role and power. Perhaps the first question should
be not, 'How do we organise the marketing department?' but, 'Do
we need a marketing department at all?'. After all, firms have been
in business successfully for decades or even centuries without one.

In a small firm, this may be just a matter of titles. The important
thing is that someone is doing the marketing job, not what they are
called. It may be the managing director, or the sales manager; but
the thinking must be done and must influence company policy.
Beyond that, the process must be managed, as it will not happen
on its own.

As with any organisational task, the company must check that
the things that need to be done are defined, and that each is
assigned to a named person. Historically, since marketing has
arrived relatively recently and has been seen as something you do
to products after they have been made, the tasks have often been
seen as belonging to the sales function. Firms can be thought of as
moving through stages of development.

■ *Production oriented*: the product and its technology are central to
  the firm, and all decisions are referred back to manufacturing
  concerns.
■ *Sales oriented*: the company accepts that there are competitors and

that major efforts need to be put into promoting and selling the products; however, the products are still designed and made by reference to the firm's own criteria (think of the British clearing banks).

■ *Market oriented*: customers' and consumers' needs influence what products are made and their specifications, as well as their selling and distribution.

Where the firm is in this development will shape how it organises marketing. In the early stages, marketing will appear, if at all, as a service within sales. Later, it may be a separate department, but its influence may be limited to promotion and advertising. As it becomes more powerful, it will add other tasks, and will influence higher-level decisions on product range and even company mission. Its size and importance will grow, and the status and power of its managers will increase. Some typical organisation charts showing marketing functions are shown in Figure 1.2.

Here we need to introduce an idea which will be explored in more detail in Chapter 6: the difference between a product and a brand.

■ The brand is the totality of the company's specific product offering as perceived by customers and consumers.

We are all familiar with well-known brands such as Persil or Mars; there are also brands in other fields, such as IBM in computers or Forte in hotels. This has led to the development of the brand manager system, in which an individual manager is given responsibility for co-ordination of all the activities which affect the final delivery of the brand: market research, product formulation, packaging, advertising, promotion, distribution and so on. In some firms, the brand manager achieves power and status, and there is no doubt that having a single mind concentrating on a brand's development has many advantages. It can also lead to conflicts with other departments (see below).

Life does not stand still, however, and even as some firms are adopting marketing departments and brand manager systems, other influences seem to be challenging the solution. Briefly, three trends are apparent which will affect how the marketing function is organised in future.

Figure 1.2 Marketing organisation

1   No marketing function

| Sales | Production | Finance | Personnel |

2   Marketing as service to sales

| Sales | Production | Finance | Personnel |
| Marketing | | | |

3   Marketing as part of sales

| Sales & Marketing | Production | Finance | Personnel |

4   Separate marketing function

| Marketing | Sales | Production | Finance | Personnel |

5   Sales as part of marketing

| Marketing | Production | Finance | Personnel |
| Sales | | | |

6   Possible marketing department

Marketing director

| Sales | Advertising & promotion | Market research | Planning & stats |

7   Brand management system

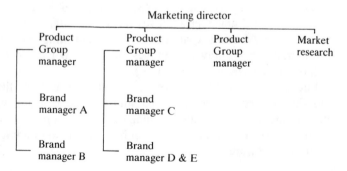

Marketing director

Product Group manager	Product Group manager	Product Group manager	Market research
Brand manager A	Brand manager C		
Brand manager B	Brand manager D & E		

■ *New technology*: the application of computers is leading to much more flexible manufacturing systems; this may decrease the need for marketing to define product specification, since most customer needs can be met exactly without loss of production efficiency.

■ *International competition*: firms operating in many markets now need to face competitors who are making decisions on a global or regional basis. To keep up, all firms will also adopt international strategies, and some major marketing decisions will therefore be made above country/company level.

■ *Increasing retailer power*: in many markets, retailer multiples have gained enormous market share and buying power. The old dominance by large manufacturers has disappeared, and firms need to adopt new strategies and structures to survive.

These factors all tend to decrease the power of the marketing department (at country level anyway). How they affect an individual firm will obviously vary, but the demands on organisation structure suggest three things:

1 The absolute need for teamwork between departments, perhaps leading to the setting up of formal business teams targeted at specific parts of the market (retail multiple, market sector) and consisting of members from all major functions

2 The need for the marketing function to concentrate all its efforts on the supremely difficult task of building and sustaining major brands

3 The separating out of other tasks, currently carried out by marketing, to a customer service function (this topic is explored in more detail in Chapter 9)   ·

PROBLEMS IN IMPLEMENTING MARKETING

Some potential problems in actually implementing the marketing concept have been touched on: the conflict between what marketing sees as its role and the claims of other functions; the changing pressures of the marketplace, competition and technology; the difficulty of really making the customer and consumer the central focus of the firm.

Some conflict between departments is inevitable, since each has its own specialisation and therefore objectives. Typically, marketing is seen as extravagant in its demands. From operations (manufacturing or service delivery), it asks for specifications and varieties to meet customer needs which detract from the efficiencies which standardisation of products or services can deliver. From finance, it asks for large sums to be invested in activities which produce, to accountants' eyes, little or no return in the short term; it may also ask for inventory levels or credit terms which will please customers but which cost the firm dearly.

All these lead to the central problem of making marketing thinking work in the company. As Nigel Piercy has pointed out (Piercy 1992) most companies will agree with the proposition that long-term customer satisfaction is the desired goal.

■ Only by providing products and services which deliver long-term customer satisfaction will the firm achieve the sales and profits which will ensure survival, adequate earnings per share, return on capital and all the other desirable objectives.

■ Yet hardly any company actually measures, on a regular and systematic basis, the level of customer satisfaction being achieved; virtually no-one uses such measures to drive reward systems or decide how to run the business.

The reason for this odd paradox is that to be truly market led is extremely difficult. It demands new ways of thinking and acting throughout the company, and probably new ways of organising and of measuring results. Some firms achieve it, and are successful on most business measures as a result. This is easiest to see in retailing, where such companies such as Marks & Spencer or The Body Shop consistently outperform their competitors. In such firms, it is common for the primacy of the consumer to be recognised at all levels and functions; everyone, from board directors down (or up, depending on one's point of view), spend time and effort keeping up to date with changing tastes. Similar efforts are seen in industrial companies, in which visits to customer plants by staff from various departments keep everyone in touch.

This does not imply that marketing is the only secret, or the most important function. Marks & Spencer are formidably good at specifying and controlling quality from their suppliers; Procter & Gamble, the US multi-national which is a leading force in many world markets with brands such as Fairy Liquid and Pampers, is formidably good at manufacturing products to a consistently high standard.

The important thing is that the idea of customer satisfaction is recognised throughout the company as paramount, and that the difficulties involved in delivering that are recognised and faced up to.

A good start is to insist that senior managers from every department have some regular customer contact, as Marks & Spencer do. This should percolate through all levels, so that everyone has some recent, fresh experience of what customers actually think of what we are doing for them. There may be some unpleasant surprises, but hopefully some pleasant ones as well.

The second way of overcoming marketing problems is that mentioned earlier, of teamwork. Although it can appear a truism, it is more and more vital that everyone appreciates the fundamental fact that the firm faces common problems which will be solved only by common solutions – by teamwork and breaking down departmental barriers.

MARKETING IN DIFFERENT CONTEXTS

So far we have talked only of companies, and mainly of products. How far can the marketing concept be applied in other contexts, outside the field of consumer goods?

Products and services

First, it should be said that the term product is used in this book as shorthand for products and services. In most advanced countries, services now account for much more of the national wealth than manufactured products. In reality, most firms deliver a mix of the two. There is a spectrum from pure physical product to pure service (Figure 1.3), but there are few firms at the extreme ends of the scale. In many industries, the service element is becoming more important even where the physical product is dominant, especially in providing a competitive edge.

In theory, marketing principles apply whatever the product/ service mix. It is usually said that services differ from physical products in that they are:

■ *Intangible*: it is therefore more difficult to describe and communicate the benefits of our offering.

Figure 1.3 The product–service spectrum

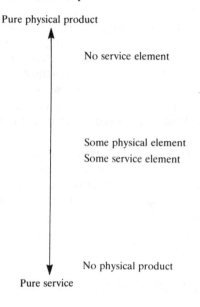

Pure physical product

No service element

Some physical element
Some service element

No physical product

Pure service

- *Inseparable*: the 'product' comes into existence only at the moment of purchase.
- *Variable* (or heterogeneous): it is delivered by different people at different times, and therefore cannot be subject to the same strict quality control as physical products.
- *Perishable*: a service cannot be stored. A theatre or airline seat unfilled today is lost forever.
- Finally, *ownership* is not transferred: we rent a hotel room for a limited period, but the ownership remains with the proprietor.

What all this means in practice is that operations and marketing become even more inextricably entwined than they ought to be (but usually are not) in manufacturing. To the four Ps of product marketing – Product, Price, Promotion, Place (see Chapter 5) – are added a further three: People, Process and Physical Evidence. All must still be geared to making the most of the match between the company, the customers and competitors, and to delivering a sustainable competitive advantage. This argument applies as forcibly to professional services such as accountants or lawyers as

to consumer services, though there may be additional complications due to ethical or legal considerations.

Consumer and industrial marketing

Marketing practice has developed mostly in consumer markets,
and is still most obvious there. Industrial markets (or business-to-
business markets) are sometimes seen to be different, and to
demand a different approach.

While it is true that marketing heavy engineering plant is
different from marketing confectionery, it is also true that there is
a great deal of overlap between the sectors. Not only are some
products (cars, detergents) bought by both consumers and organisations, but some consumer markets are characterised by large,
relatively expensive, infrequent purchases (furniture, stereo
systems) while some industrial markets are made up of frequent
purchases of small items (stationery, consumable supplies).

Having said that, most industrial markets are somewhat
different from most consumer markets. Industrial markets usually
have the following features:

- *Long-term relationships* between supplier and buyer
- *Complexity of product*
- *Complexity of buying process*
- *Greater dominance of the technical function* in the supplier (and
  therefore lesser influence of marketing)

Other features often found are:

- Purchases are usually less frequent.
- The average price per transaction is much higher.
- An industrial product may be more crucial to the buyer's business,
  which may depend on it for successful performance.
- Reciprocity of buying is often a feature of the relationship.
- Sellers may service a wide range of very different markets, each
  with different needs and buying processes.
- These different markets may react differently to the elements of
  the marketing mix (see Chapter 5).
- Manufacturers may need to understand not just their immediate
  market, but several levels, perhaps as far as end users.

Many of these differences centre round the buying process, and it is vital in industrial marketing to understand this thoroughly; Chapter 3 looks at this aspect.

In many ways, I have argued for some years, industrial and consumer marketing are converging. Marketers of consumer goods are having to adopt the industrial marketing discipline of managing a long-term relationship with a few powerful buyers, because of the rise of dominant retailers. Many industrial marketers, on the other hand, are learning from their consumer colleagues the techniques of brand-building.

The lesson must be to understand your particular market thoroughly, using the analytical approach developed in this book, and to develop solutions relevant to your firm and its situation.

Not-for-profit organisations

As more and more previously public sector organisations are being exposed to market pressures, either directly through privatisation or indirectly through such mechanisms as internal markets or competitive tendering, the applicability of marketing to non-commercial situations is being debated.

Some writers have tried to widen the definition of marketing to include almost any human transaction, but there is a danger that such definitions become so broad as to be meaningless. Clearly, there is a potential benefit to any organisation in trying to define who its customers are, what their current and emerging needs are, and how the organisation might best meet those needs within its own set of objectives and constraints.

What must be recognised is that, for most such organisations, these objectives and constraints contain explicit or implicit political dimensions. For example, the National Health Service or the police force cannot apply the marketing concept completely. For the NHS, demand is infinite but resources are not; it is simply impossible for the service to give everyone what they want (or need, which may be different). The police, to meet their objectives, sometimes have to give at least some of their 'customers' what they actively do not want.

Thus it is again a case of trying the ideas out on your own particular situation, to see what benefit they might provide. Taking a marketing view may at the very least open up fresh perspectives; it may also help in ordering priorities for action.

THE APPROACH OF THIS BOOK

This book takes you through each phase of the marketing approach to business problems, providing a way of tackling each. The approach developed will not guarantee to give you the right answer to every problem, but it will offer a good chance of coming up with a well thought through analysis and a sound solution.

We start in Chapters 2 and 3 by looking at the things outside the organisation which we cannot control but which will impact on our activities. Chapter 2 examines the environment, markets and competitors; Chapter 3 goes on to deal with how to understand customers and consumers.

In Chapter 4 we tackle the fundamental question of marketing information: what information do we need, and how do we go about finding it.

We then move back inside the firm in Chapter 5 to look at the things we *can* control – the marketing mix. Subsequent chapters then take each element of the mix in turn: existing products and new products; setting the price; communicating with markets; and distributing the products.

Finally, in Chapter 10, we put everything together and tackle marketing strategy and planning.

USING THE WORKSHEETS

In each chapter, you will find worksheets for you to fill in. The purpose is to help you apply the ideas outlined in the chapter to your own situation; in this way you will really understand the concepts and be able to test each to see if it will really work for you.

Try to tackle each worksheet as you go through, even if it is only roughly. Some are quite simple (though they all demand some careful thought); others may take more time and effort, for example in finding information about your organisation, its markets and customers; these you may need to come back to and spend more time on.

They are all designed to help *you.* If a particular worksheet is too difficult, or does not fit your particular situation, pass over it quickly as long as you have absorbed the main points of the argument. Their value will be apparent both at the level of each chapter, and – most of all – when you come to putting them all together to produce a marketing plan at the end.

2 Understanding what we can't control

Environments, markets, competitors

We saw in the first chapter that marketing's unique role is to look outside the business. In this chapter we will start to examine how to put marketing into practice by looking at the first part of that process: analysing the environment, the firm's markets, and competitors. Chapter 3 will go on to look at customers and consumers, and in the rest of the book we will see how to adapt the firm's policies to what we have seen in the world outside.

ENVIRONMENTS

The word environment has in recent years come to have a specific meaning – the physical environment, and all the 'Green' issues surrounding it. Here we use it to include not only that, but all aspects of the world in which the organisation exists, and which affects its future. 'No man is an island', nor is a firm; it lives in a complex set of surroundings in a particular society at a particular time, and it must understand that context in order to adapt to it most effectively.

At this level, marketing overlaps with the broader corporate strategy, since the environment can have effects on the firm outside the purely marketing area; for instance, legislation on health and safety, or financial reporting, will affect what the firm does. Here, we are concerned only with marketing, but the other areas should not be forgotten.

Each organisation will be affected in different ways by different parts of its environment. A handy summary of these different parts is PEST: political, economic, social, technological. Each firm needs to analyse which environmental effects are of most relevance to its markets. For some, such as machine tool manufacturers or building societies, economic factors will be highly relevant; while for others, such as cosmetics manufacturers or health clubs, social and attitudinal change will be more important.

A brief comment will be given on each area to provide some idea of likely factors to take into account. When you have read this, try to fill in Worksheet 2.1, identifying the PEST factors most relevant to your company, to your major customers, and to their markets. In identifying factors, try to look beyond today, and see what trends are visible, what is likely to be happening over the next five to ten years (depending on how long your company's planning

WORKSHEET 2.1 ENVIRONMENTAL FACTORS

■ List the environmental factors relevant to your company under each heading and note the impact on yourself, your major customers and their markets.

		Impact	
Factors	*Your company*	*Main customers*	*Their markets*
Political/legal			
Economic			
Social/cultural			
Technological			

horizon is – that is, how long it will take you to react to a given change, by building a new plant or developing a new brand or model, for example).

Political/legal

Some years ago, Hoffmann La Roche, the Swiss pharmaceutical company, refused to bow to UK government pressure to reduce the prices of two of its major drugs. When the government later introduced a list of drugs which could no longer be prescribed on the National Health Service, these two best sellers were on the list, and the company lost half its UK sales as a result. Such insensitivity to the political environment was catastrophic. How sensitive is your industry to political change? Recent government policies have had dramatic effects on, for example, the brewing industry; other investigations may result in changes for CD manufacturers and publishers.

Both in the political and the resulting field of legislation, a careful eye needs to be kept on not only the UK government, but on supra-national bodies, in particular the European Communities. Do you know what the European Commission is thinking about your industry and your markets?

Economic

If your markets are sensitive to the economic cycle, then you need to have as good an understanding of economic factors as possible. When even the government is incapable of forecasting economic trends accurately, this may seem a counsel of perfection; but even a thorough reading of the commentaries in newspapers such as the *Financial Times* and the *Economist* will help to ensure that you have some idea of the direction the economy is taking, so that you can prepare yourself.

Of course, if your sales are not much affected by economic changes, do not bother; information which is not used is a waste of time and money.

Social/cultural

For many marketing people, factors affecting how we live our lives are likely to be the most interesting. Some of these are objective facts, and easy to establish. The size of the different age groups in the population, for instance, is known fairly exactly, and can be predicted for almost all groups for the next five and ten years, since all the relevant people are already born. It is known that there was a sharp dip in the late-teens–early-twenties age group at the beginning of the 1990s; we are also seeing a growth of the over-fifty population, a decline in traditional two-parent-two-children households and an increase in single-parent and single-person units. Such changes mean new opportunities for some firms, and perhaps a re-ordering of priorities for others.

Other social and cultural factors are harder to pin down. Some, such as changes in eating habits (more snacking, fewer formal family eating occasions) can be measured by market research. Others, such as changing attitudes to brands (see Chapter 6) are more difficult to measure exactly. The most difficult task is to distinguish a fad from a continuing trend; all the marketer can do is to try to understand the underlying causes of change and make a judgement. This is an area in which flair counts for a lot.

Technological

Although this may seem outside the marketing remit, it is important that marketing people keep an eye on developments which may affect their markets. Some markets have been dramatically affected by technological change, the best-known example being the Swiss watch industry. Until electronic watches came along, the Swiss dominated the world market for watch movements. Early electronic watches were expensive, clumsy and not very functional; the Swiss dismissed them and carried on making their mechanical movements. As we now know, they were wrong, and they suffered drastic losses from which they have recovered only partially.

This story is typical of much technological change, in that the innovation came from outside the industry, and its effects were difficult to predict; in particular, consumer acceptance of the new products was very tricky to forecast in the early days. Taking a broad view of new technologies (particularly electronics and bio-technology), and looking at the world as a whole, what may change your markets over the next ten years?

MARKETS

The next stage down in scale is to examine the markets in which your products are sold. The first thing to do is to define the markets, one at a time. This may seem rather obvious, but what constitutes our market is not quite as straightforward as may at first appear. How we define the market affects how we see our buyers and potential buyers, our market share, our competitors. More importantly, it may affect how we see our relative success and failure, and our future.

Most firms define their markets in terms of their products: the market for hamburgers, or retail banking, or fractional horsepower electric motors. This has the advantage of simplicity, and makes definition and perhaps measurement easy. From a marketing point of view, it may obscure important insights.

■ The chairman of Carborundum, an American firm which used to specialise in making carborundum grinding wheels, re-defined his view of the market by saying, 'Our customers don't want grinding wheels; they want metal removed'. Defining the market in terms of *customer needs* can open up whole new vistas of opportunity.

A market, to a marketing person, is a group of people with certain needs. These needs may or not be met at present; or they may be met with greater or less success by the products and services on offer, from our firm and from others. Our task is to define those people and their needs, and to find ways of meeting those needs better than anyone else.

Start, then, with the people who are currently buying your products, and define the needs which you are meeting. It may be helpful to start with only one or two products, those which account for most of your sales and profits. Use Worksheet 2.2, and fill in who the buyers are, what the needs are, and what other products meet the same need. Use two levels of definition: a very broad one (such as food, for a restaurant chain), and a narrower one (such as convenience food within the city centre).

This leads to a consideration of *served market*: that portion of the total market which we are trying to operate in. Few firms try to cover the whole of a market; even very large companies such as the major car manufacturers do not compete in every sector of the market. From the definition we can calculate the total market in which we are competing, and our share. Do this in Worksheet 2.3.

The worksheet asks you to fill in (or estimate) the figures for

WORKSHEET 2.2 DEFINING MARKETS

| Product | Who buys | Need met by product | | Other products which meet need |
		Broad	Narrow	

five years ago, this year and next year. The point of this is not to spend large amounts of time and effort on exact numbers, but to give a view of trends in the market. Are the markets going up, or down, or are they more or less stable? Are your shares of the markets going up or down? It is vital to take this dynamic view, since markets rarely stay the same for long. Even if your sales are stable or indeed growing, you may be losing share, or growing share of a declining market. A blinkered view of markets may seriously mislead you as to your current success and future prospects.

Here we will introduce a piece of marketing jargon: the Product Life Cycle. This idea suggests that products are like living creatures, and go through the stages of birth, growth, maturity, decline and death. Figure 2.1 shows the product life cycle, labelled with the terms normally used in marketing: introduction, growth, maturity and decline (other terms are sometimes used, but the concept is the same). Using your knowledge of your markets, try plotting your major products on the PLC.

WORKSHEET 2.3 MARKET TRENDS AND SHARES

Products or product groups

	1	2	3	4
Name of product:	___	___	___	___

Definition of served market
  (e.g. fast food in city centre, or wholesalers of £10–20 million turnover)

Total market (£)
  5 years ago
  This year
  Next year

Our sales (£)
  5 years ago
  This year
  Next year

Our share
  5 years ago
  This year
  Next year

Comments

Figure 2.1 The product life cycle

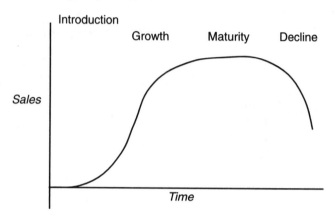

Figure 2.2 shows a view of what market conditions are likely to obtain in the different stages of the cycle. Compare what the chart says about market conditions with your experience of your markets: does it sound familiar, and what does it tell you about the way the market may develop?

It is fair to say that there is some controversy in marketing about the use of the PLC. In some markets, the phenomenon is clearly visible. In my life time, for example, the electronic calculator has moved rapidly from a large, cumbersome, expensive, desktop machine made by only a few manufacturers, through an explosive growth stage with many new competitors and models and falling prices, to a consolidation stage in which many manufacturers have dropped out, and the technology and price levels have stabilised. Other markets, on the other hand, have been in a more or less stable condition for many years, and it is less clear what the PLC concept has to offer.

A refinement of the idea distinguishes between the product class, product form, and brand. In the case of a stable market such as bread, the product class is all bread, the product form whole-meal bread, and a brand Hovis. The shape of the cycle may be different for these different elements.

The major lesson for anyone trying to understand their markets is that change is inevitable. The PLC may give you fresh insights,

Figure 2.2 What happens in the different stages of the product life cycle

	Phase			
Characteristics	*Introduction*	*Growth*	*Maturity*	*Decline*
Sales	Low sales	Rapidly rising sales	Peak sales	Declining sales
Costs	High cost per customer	Average cost per customer	Low cost per customer	Low cost per customer
Profits	Negative	Rising profits	High profits	Declining profits
Customers	Innovators	Early adopters	Middle majority	Laggards
Competitors	Few	Growing number	Stable number beginning to decline	Declining number

Marketing objectives

	Create product awareness and trial	Maximise market share	Maximise profit while defending market share	Reduce expenditure and milk the brand

Strategies

Product	Offer a basic product	Offer product extensions, service warranty	Diversify brands and models	Phase out weak items
Price	Use cost-plus	Price to penetrate market	Price to match or beat competitors	Cut price
Distribution	Build selective distribution	Build intensive distribution	Build more intensive distribution	Go selective: phase out unprofitable outlets
Advertising	Build product awareness among early adopters and dealers	Build awareness and interest in the mass market	Stress brand differences and benefits	Reduce to level needed to retain hardcore loyals
Sales promotion	Use heavy sales promotion to entice trial	Reduce to take advantage of heavy consumer demand	Increase to encourage brand switching	Reduce to minimal level

Sources: Chester R. Wasson (1978) *Dynamic Competitive Strategies and Product Life Cycles*, Austin, TX: Austin Press; John A. Weber (1976) 'Planning corporate growth with inverted product life cycles', *Long Range Planning*, October: 12–29; Peter Doyle (1976) 'The realities of the product life cycle', *Quarterly Review of Marketing*, Summer: 1–6. Adapted from Kotler (1991: 367).

but like any other management tool, it will not give easy answers as to what you should do in any particular circumstances.

Let us now move on from the market as a whole to our position in it. You have defined (or estimated) your market share. This is important because of a large body of evidence that market share has a central effect on profitability. Various pieces of research suggest that the number one brand in a market is the most profitable, the second brand rather less so, and most other brands unprofitable. Obviously, scale gives the potential for many economies, and all other things being equal, the biggest manufacturer ought to have the lowest costs; low costs give the opportunity for higher margins to invest in further product development, in advertising support, or for price wars.

As with all findings in business research, there are exceptions to and disagreements with this simple statement. Some firms with small shares are very profitable, and not all firms with the largest share make the most profit. Nevertheless, the relationship between share and profit is a powerful one. In many consumer markets, the growing power of retailers means that being number one or two brand in a category may be absolutely essential to survival, as all other brands may be de-listed by the multiples.

The discussion underlines the importance of market definition referred to earlier, as changing the definition of your served market can change your apparent market share, and therefore your conclusions about the profit you should be making. This leads on to the idea of market structure. Using Worksheet 2.4, build up a picture of your firm within its market, compared with competitors. Again, use estimates if you do not have exact figures. You may have to use different market definitions if figures are available for a broad market but not for a narrower sector of it. Fill in both volume and value for sales, as they may show different pictures. Try to get or estimate profits, even though that may be difficult.

Most markets have a structure with a clear leader, second and third; frequently the profitability of the competitors follows their size. If it does not in your case, can you think of reasons why?

In many markets, the participants operate in different *strategic groups.* In the washing-up liquid market, for example, there are a few major national (or multi-national) manufacturers selling major national brands supported by heavy advertising, and another group making own-label products for retailers, some selling locally or

WORKSHEET 2.4 MARKET STRUCTURE, SHARE AND PROFITS

■ Take your whole firm, or just one of its major products, and list your sales and profits compared with your direct competitors in that market. Use estimates if you do not have exact figures.

	Sales vol.	Sales (£)	Share (%)	Profit	Share of profit
Our firm or product					
Competitor A					
Competitor B					
Competitor C					
All others					
Total market					

---

regionally and without advertising. These are distinct strategic groups, and firms in one cannot be compared directly with those in another. Are there strategic groups in your industry? Which do you belong to, and is it the most profitable?

WORKSHEET 2.5 IDENTIFYING CURRENT AND FUTURE
COMPETITORS

■ Take your major products or product groups, and
identify the main competitors. Then go on to think of
other firms who may compete with you in future, even
from right outside your present industry (for example,
tele-conferencing may compete with airlines if it replaces
some business travel).

Our major products/
product groups

Name: _____ _____ _____ _____

1 Current
  competitors

2 New
  competitors
  from same
  market
    UK

    Europe

    Other
    countries

3 New
  competitors
  from other
  fields and
  technologies

COMPETITORS

You should be very aware of who your main competitors are; if not, the exercises so far in this chapter should have helped to identify them. As Chapter 1 made clear, it is marketing's job not only to meet the needs of the market, but also to do so better than competitors. Most markets today are highly competitive, and becoming more so; keeping an eye on competitors, foreseeing their likely moves, and counteracting them, are vital parts of the management task.

Compare the last column of Worksheet 2.2 (Other products which meet the need) with the competitors listed in Worksheet 2.4. Are they the same, or do you need to re-think your definition of the competition? Remembering the example of the Swiss watch industry, it is vital to take an open view of who may be competing in our markets in future. The opening up of markets (as in Europe), the rapid advance of technology in many fields, and the drive of ambitious companies into new areas of business, all mean that current definitions of competition will almost certainly be out of date in a few years.

Using Worksheet 2.5, list current competitors, and try to identify potential new entrants from abroad and from other fields. What will the Japanese be doing? the other South-east Asian nations such as Taiwan, Singapore and Korea? China? Other nations?

Having identified the main competitors, the next step is to understand them. Most firms have a great deal of knowledge of their competitors, but it is not always brought together in one place. It is helpful to have a dossier on each, either on paper or in the computer, and to encourage everyone to contribute to it and keep it up to date. Sales, product and financial information are basic, but other information on likely future moves is also key. A useful way of summarising this sort of data is a SWOT analysis. Chapter 10 on planning will return to this technique, but at this stage it might be useful to try a SWOT for yourself and your major competitor, using Worksheet 2.6.

Taking all the Worksheets you have completed for this chapter, you should now have a clearer view of:

■ The major environmental factors likely to affect your firm

WORKSHEET 2.6 SWOT ANALYSIS

> ■ Copy this sheet, or better still use a flip chart, and fill in for your own company and for your major competitor.
> ■ Things *internal* to the company are strengths and weaknesses.
> ■ Things *external* to the company are opportunities and threats.
>
>
> | *Strengths* | *Weaknesses* |
> |---|---|
> | | |
> | *Opportunities* | *Threats* |

■ What markets you are in
■ Who your buyers are in those markets
■ The needs your products are meeting
■ Your market share
■ The directions the markets and your shares are moving in
■ Who are your main competitors, and their strengths and weaknesses
■ What potential new competitors may emerge

In the next chapter we will go on to look in more detail at your customers and consumers.

3 Understanding customers and consumers

The most important people in our world

Since meeting the needs of the marketplace is central to a firm's survival, identifying current and future customers and consumers, and defining their needs, must be central to marketing's task. In this chapter we will look first at customers, that is organisations which are buying for their own use or for re-sale; then at consumers, that is, individuals buying for their own or their family's consumption.

CUSTOMERS

Every firm has customers, whether or not their goods or services are eventually bought by individual consumers. For those who are engaged entirely in industrial or business-to-business marketing, customers should be the centre and focus of all activity. Even those firms who market to consumers have to sell through retailers and wholesalers, and these customers are increasingly important. So, how do we go about understanding these people?

The first stage is to identify them. This may seem over-obvious; after all, we all know who our customers are, don't we? The answer is that we certainly ought to, but that it is not always true that we do. If you have only a handful of customers, you probably know them well; but most firms have a reasonably large number of customers, and many have only a vague idea who they are. The 80/20 rule applies here, as in other areas of business:

■ A very large proportion of your business (say 80 per cent) is probably accounted for by a relatively small proportion (say 20 per cent) of your customers.

WORKSHEET 3.1 IDENTIFYING CUSTOMERS

■   Identify the most important of your customers in terms of sales. This may mean the top five, or the top twenty or more, depending on your situation.

	Purchased from us		% of our sales	
	This year £'000	*Last year £'000*	*This year*	*Last year*
Customer				
1				
2				
3				
4				
5				
All others				
Total				

As a first step, then, list your largest customers in Worksheet 3.1, with the proportion of your total sales they account for. In a large or complicated company you may have to do this by product group or industry; in this case, use Worksheet 3.2 to summarise the pattern. The idea in either case is to focus on the main sources of your business currently, with two major purposes:

1   to draw broad conclusions on where the business is and where it is going

WORKSHEET 3.2 CUSTOMERS BY INDUSTRY/PRODUCT GROUP

■ Use this worksheet if you sell to several different industries; if you sell only to one industry (or to consumers), and have only one product group, you may want to go straight on to Worksheet 3.3. List customers and the percentage of your total sales accounted for by each, classified by your product groups and the industry of the customers, e.g. Bloggs Tools buys our Product Group A products; they are in industry 1, and their total purchases from us account for 15 per cent of our sales. An industry group might be banks, or insurance companies, or hospitals.

	Customer industry group			
	1	*2*	*3*	*4*
Our product group				
A	Bloggs 15%			
B				
C				
D				
E				

2   to provide a basis for a closer understanding of individual customers

As to the broad picture, you could ask yourself some questions:

■ Are there any surprises? Is our business coming from unexpected sources, or moving in a direction we did not realise?
■ Are we over-reliant on one or two major customers (and what would happen if they switched to another supplier)?
■ What industry or industries are we supplying?
■ Which individual customers ought we to be concentrating on now, and in the future?

On the last point, it is important to remember (without anticipating Chapter 10 on planning) that we should always be looking not only at what is happening now, but at trends and changes, so that we can focus on the future of the business and not only its past.

Studying individual customers

Let us assume that we have identified our most important customers. These may number three or four, or tens; they should account for a significant part of our total sales (though this may vary from under 50 per cent to over 80 per cent). They should reflect today's reality, and tomorrow's prospects. What do we need to know about them?

The first thing is a refinement and an inversion of what we know already:

■ How important are they to us?
■ How important are we to them?

We have already answered the first question in terms of sales, but we need to look also at profit (some would argue that we ought to have done that at the first stage, and perhaps we should – but it is also useful to start simply and introduce complications slowly). For each of your identified major customers, use Worksheet 3.3 to summarise the trend in your sales to them, and the amount of profit you make from them. If you don't know how much profit you are making from each, then this is a good time to find out.

Are there any surprises? What trends are apparent? Where is

WORKSHEET 3.3 CUSTOMER IMPORTANCE

■ List customers by the percentage of your total sales, and total profits, they account for. Use the last three years and an estimate of next year.

	% of our total sales			*% of our total profit*		
Year:	*Next 199..*	*199..*	*199..*	*Next 199..*	*199..*	*199..*
Customer						
1						
2						
3						
4						
5						
6						
7						
8						
9						

most of your *profit* coming from?

As to the second question, this requires some empathy on your part. Put yourself in your customer's shoes, and try to see your company from their point of view. What exactly are you supplying them? There are two aspects to this: quantitative and qualitative. The quantitative one can in theory be answered fairly simply: what proportion of their total purchases are from your firm? The qualitative aspect comes from the answer to the question, 'How important is your product or service to the customer's business?'

For example, you may supply a small component which accounts for a fairly small proportion of total purchases by the customer; but the performance of their product may depend vitally on your component. Equally, the quality of what you supply, or the reliability of delivery, may be absolutely crucial. Use Worksheet 3.4 to summarise how important your firm is to each major customer.

From this understanding of the nature of the relationship between the two organisations, you can build up a more detailed picture of each customer. It is helpful to have as much hard information as possible, for example, published accounts.

WORKSHEET 3.4 HOW IMPORTANT ARE WE TO OUR CUSTOMERS

■ Give both a quantitative estimate (what percentage of their purchases in this product field do we account for) and a qualitative view (how much difference do we make to their successful performance).

■ Fill in a sheet for each major customer.

*Customer*_____

	% of their total purchases in this field	*Comments on importance*
Our product		
1		
2		
3		
4		
5		
6		

Although these often hide as much as they reveal, a good analysis can tell you quite a lot about the customer and where it is heading financially. If you are not an accountant, ask your company accountant or finance department to produce an analysis for you (and explain what it means!). Try to use several years' data, since as so often it is the trends which are important rather than a static picture of one point in the past.

Beyond the financial figures, try to gauge the customer's standing in its industry, for example, its market share and its competitive position. Is it a leader or a follower? What is its overall strategy? What direction is it trying to go in?

The point of this sort of analysis is to see where our products fit in, and how we can help our customer to achieve his or her business objectives. If we are selling office stationery, then our role in our customer's overall strategy will be relatively small; but it may still be important to understand how our service fits in with that strategy (do they want glossy stationery to suit an up-market image, or a low-cost, efficient service to accord with a low-cost strategy?). If our product contributes significantly to our customer's success, then we should be working closely with them on future product development and strategy. In fact, in many industries, the trend is towards greater *partnership* between suppliers and customers as they realise that their interests are in fact common. The adversarial atmosphere in which a buyer played off competing suppliers against each other, and bargained fiercely on price, is giving way to relationships in which the two parties work together to commonly defined ends. That does not, of course, mean that competition and price are now irrelevant; but that a positive approach to understanding a customer's needs and to meeting them will lead to a more constructive relationship and, potentially, greater profits for both.

To reach this sort of relationship means building contacts with all the relevant people in the customer organisation. This is the final step in this stage, to identify the people in each major customer who are important to us. The next section looks at this in general terms; at this point, fill in the first part of Worksheet 3.5 (Who buys the product). We shall return to fill in the rest later.

Organisational buying behaviour

The major characteristic of buying by organisations is that, for most products, several people will be involved with the purchasing decision. Identifying them and their role at the different stages of the decision-making process, and deciding how to influence them, are tasks for marketing.

The range of buying decisions is vast, and obviously some will be long and complex processes while others will be routine. Generally speaking, a new purchase or purchasing situation will be more complex than one which has been carried out many times. The level of complexity will also be affected by how important the purchase is to the buying organisation; this covers not only the absolute size of the purchase, but also the part the product plays in the buyer's business, as discussed above. The more complex the decision, the more people will be involved in it.

It is helpful therefore to classify the buying decision. Is the decision to buy your product a new situation previously not encountered by your customer, a routine one met every week or month, or something in between? Quite what classification you

WORKSHEET 3.5 IMPORTANT INDIVIDUALS IN THE CUSTOMER FIRM

	Who buys	Classification of task[a]	Who influences	Role[b]
■ Fill in a sheet for each major customer.				
Our product or product group				
1				
2				
3				
4				

Notes: [a]Tasks classified by e.g. new task, mixture of new and old, routine re-purchase. [b]Roles classified by user, buyer, influencer, decider, gatekeeper.

adopt will depend on the nature of your business, but some sort of three-way split into new, mixture and routine will probably be enough.

The people involved in the buying decision will have different roles. They are often described as:

- user
- buyer
- influencer
- decider
- gatekeeper (who controls the flow of information to the others)

Sometimes one person may take several roles, perhaps at different stages of the process; equally, there may be several people contributing to one role. The people involved in a particular buying decision are called the decision-making unit; identifying the DMU is central to influencing it to buy your product.

Go back to Worksheet 3.5 and fill in the other columns, identifying where you can the members of the DMU for your various products (they may obviously vary between products).

For each person identified, the ideal is then to understand their objectives, values and motivations so that marketing effort can be geared to influencing them. This is clearly a tall order, but even to know who they are, and what their decision criteria are, is a start.

UNDERSTANDING CONSUMERS

We left the study of organisational buying behaviour at the level of the individual, and we carry on at that level with consumers. In the end, both industrial and consumer buyers are human beings, subject to the same emotions and pressures, however different the contexts. If there were a science of human behaviour we should be able to model, measure and predict what individuals and groups would do in given circumstances. Unfortunately, despite the enormous amount of time and effort expended in the study of the social sciences, we are, to be frank, not a lot further forward.

Marketing people have borrowed freely from the social sciences in their attempts to understand consumers, but little of the work has been of lasting value. Various models and methods have been touted at various times, and have had some success; but none has lasted and shown general applicability. What such techniques can offer is insights into particular marketing problems, and the reading of texts on psychology and sociology, or perhaps better, specialised books on consumer behaviour, can be useful at that level.

The literature is too vast even to attempt to summarise here, but some headings under which information may be sought are given; they are classified as relating to individual or to group influences on behaviour.

Individual influences

- *Perception*: how do we perceive information about products, through advertising, packaging etc.?
- *Information processing*: how do we process the information, through learning and forgetting, exchange, persuasion?
- *Decision-making*: how do we actually make buying decisions?
- *Motivation*: what drives our behaviour?
- *Personality*: what effect does personality type have on buying?
- *Attitudes*: what attitudes do consumers have towards our products and what effect does this have on their buying?

Group influences

- *Culture*: what are the shared values and beliefs we gain by being brought up and living in a particular country, region or group of people?
- *Social class*: what effect does social class have on buying?
- *Other group influences*: what effect do groups to which we belong – such as family, friends, work – or would like to belong – such as jet-setters, style-makers, pop stars – have on our behaviour?

The use of some of these will be returned to in the next chapter. For now, we can only note that none of the research available will give you the answer to a specific marketing problem, though they may help you structure your thinking and give you ideas.

The really useful approach is to concentrate on understanding your consumer using the simplest tools available. As with industrial buyers, we will start by identifying our consumers. You started this process in Worksheet 2.2; now we will try to refine it. Can you

WORKSHEET 3.6 IDENTIFYING CONSUMERS

■ Use any data you have about the consumers of your products, or give your educated guess for later confirmation.

	Hard data Age, sex, region, etc.	*Soft data* Feelings, preferences, etc.
Product		
1		
2		
3		
4		
5		
6		

---

describe your consumers at all specifically? Use Worksheet 3.6 to give both hard data (age, sex, region, frequency etc.) and any soft data you may have (what sort of people they are, what they feel about the products). If you have no data, this may give you a lead towards the sort of information you wish to collect; this is dealt with in the next chapter.

Having identified your consumers, the central need is to understand the role your product plays in their lives. As with industrial products, consumer products cover a range of buying and using situations. Some are low-involvement products which we buy often at low cost and with little thought; others we buy very rarely, spend a lot of money on, and invest time and effort in choosing. It may help, therefore, to start by classifying what sort of product yours is.

As with industrial products, there are many ways to classify, and you will have to work out what is best for you. One way would be based on purchase frequency and price:

- ■ Frequently bought, low price
- ■ Moderate frequency and price
- ■ Infrequently bought, high price

Another might be a related view of how much effort goes into the buying process:

- ■ Low involvement, bought at any of many outlets, little thought
- ■ Some searching, moderate amount of involvement in choice
- ■ High involvement, lots of searching and comparison

The important thing is whether your classification tells you anything useful about your consumers or the marketing process. What the approach should do is to lead you towards the central idea of this section, which is the absolute necessity of understanding the *product-in-use*. This means understanding how the product fits into your consumers' lives, what problems they are

WORKSHEET 3.7 CONSUMERS AND OUR PRODUCTS

■ Again, use existing information if you have it, or educated guesses which you may want to test by later research.		
	Type of purchase[a]	*Role of product in use* '*I use this to ...*'
Our product		
1		
2		
3		
4		

Note: [a]Type of purchase classified by e.g. frequent purchase, low involvement; moderate involvement, some search; high involvement, significant effort.

trying to solve in buying and using, what are their objectives and criteria (explicit and hidden).

This is an extension of the idea in Chapter 2 of describing the needs your product is meeting, and of the normal marketing way of asking what the benefits are that your product is delivering. It is vital to grasp this idea of product-in-use, since so much of what passes for marketing thinking seems to concentrate on other aspects (such as advertising, or attitudes to the brand) while ignoring what consumers actually do with the product.

Using Worksheet 3.7, classify your products by type (if this is helpful), and put as much effort as you can into a specific description of the role your product plays in consumers' lives. We shall return in Chapter 6 to an examination of what a product is, but at this stage you may find it useful to list different roles, for example, the functional role ('Persil washes clothes') and other life roles ('Using Persil gives me confidence that I am caring for my family in the best way I can'). If you can understand and apply this central idea (better than your competitors) you will have made the most important step in understanding and applying marketing.

4 Information for marketing

What do we need to know and how do we find out?

Information is of particular importance to marketing managers. In the last chapters we have looked at the influences outside the firm which marketing people must take account of. In all cases, they need information to find out what is going on: information about trends in the environment, about markets, competitors, customers and consumers.

In the days when each shopkeeper or craftsman knew all the customers personally, the information was available through direct knowledge. That is still true to an extent, and perhaps in these more sophisticated days it is worth remembering that direct personal contact with customers and consumers is invaluable. Beyond the few personal contacts that any individual can make, however, there are large areas where the professional marketing manager needs to make sure that good information is readily available.

THE NEED FOR AND USES OF INFORMATION

In marketing, as in other areas of management, information is used for three main purposes:

- diagnosis
- decision making
- control

In the first case, diagnosis, consider the situation where sales are below target. The thoughtful manager will want to analyse the problem to identify the cause before taking any remedial action.

Thinking through that process will help us to see what information would be useful. First, one would try to identify the problem more closely.

- Are sales down for all products, or just one?
- Are sales down in all regions and customers?
- Have any of the assumptions made in the sales forecast changed?
- Have any unexpected changes happened in the environment or our markets?
- Have competitors taken any specific actions, such as launching a new product, lowering their price etc.?

Much of the information needed to make this sort of diagnosis would be readily available, but not all of it would necessarily be to hand unless the manager had previously arranged for it – for example, by making sure that sales statistics were analysed by product within region, or by ensuring that sales people's call reports were summarised and reported to management.

For making decisions, too, we need information. Any decision is a choice between different courses of action: what type and brand of stereo system to buy for our home, or what marketing action to take in a particular situation. Logically, as Figure 4.1 shows, we ought to proceed by defining what our objectives are: what exactly are we trying to achieve? In a business situation, this may be a market-share target, or sales volume, or profit – but it must be clear exactly what we are aiming at, or the choice cannot be made rationally. From the objectives can be derived specific criteria, and then we can compare the possible options against the criteria. We may already have the neccessary information to be able to make this comparison, or we may have to go out and collect it; when we have enough information, we can make our choice.

To take the previous example further, suppose that we have diagnosed the problem as having been caused by the action of a competitor, who has reduced the price of their brand. The options open to us are to meet the price reduction, to improve the amount or quality of our brand, or to introduce a special offer. In order to make the decision as to which is best, we have first to make clear what our objectives are. These are likely to be a combination of profit, sales and market-share targets. Unfortunately, some of

Figure 4.1 Information and decision making

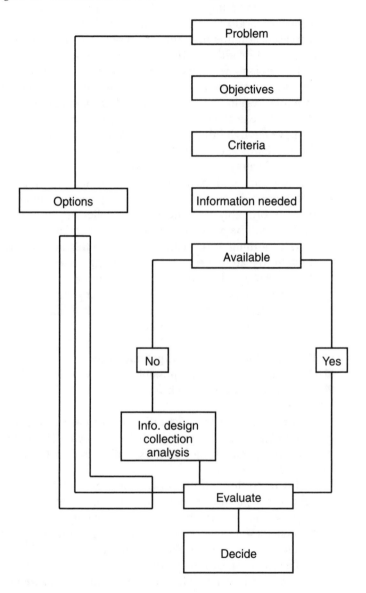

these may conflict amongst themselves, as management have a habit of demanding that both short-term and long-term profit be safeguarded at the same time as sales and share are maintained or increased. Frequently, this is impossible, and some short-term sacrifice of profit is needed to maintain market share.

Let us assume, however, that clear objectives can be defined, and that from them we can set up some specific criteria; for example, regain lost sales volume and maintain last year's market share. We can then start to compare the options, and see whether we have enough information. We obviously need estimates of what the results of each option would be in terms of sales and market share. We may be able to make these estimates on the basis of existing data and past experience, or we may feel that further information is needed. Unfortunately, in the situation outlined, there is probably no time to start collecting information, so the decision will be made on the basis of hunch and experience. While there is nothing intrinsically wrong with this, it is hardly ideal, and it ought to lead to a search for something better. How this might be done is discussed in the rest of this chapter.

Not all marketing decisions need complicated information. To choose between different media in which to place advertising, for example, you might want to know:

■ Precise definition of the target audience
■ Audience of each of the possible media vehicles
■ Cost of advertising in each

A comparison of the cost-efficiency of each media vehicle could then be made, and the most efficient chosen. (The situation is a bit more complicated than that, as is discussed in Chapter 8, but the principle is clear.)

Try to go through the process of deciding what information you need for a particular marketing decision that has arisen in your organisation, or which may be coming up in the future, using Worksheet 4.1. The objectives should generate the criteria, which should in turn generate the exact information required.

The final use of information listed above was control. We need information on what is happening outside so that we know that we still have control of events, and that our plans are working out as we had hoped. Without feedback information, we have no idea

WORKSHEET 4.1 INFORMATION FOR DECISION MAKING

Definition of marketing problem (e.g. sales of our major service are below target)

Possible options (actions to be taken)

1

2

3

Objectives (e.g. profit, increased brand awareness, market share)

Information needed to make decision

---

how things are going; even if we have no proper planning system as such, we probably have a budget, and so we need to know how we are doing against budget, at the very least. Such control information is likely to be based on sales, but may include market share, and other objectives such as increasing distribution in a particular channel or improving the consumer acceptance of a brand. The objectives should again define the information which is required.

In reality, marketing information is also used for other purposes, just as other types of information are. These purposes are political, or to protect a manager's position, or even for comfort. It is as well to be aware of these, and to accept that they exist. In an ideal world, all managers would be rational creatures operating only for the best for others and for the organisation. In the mean time, it may be worth looking at the underlying reason for collecting certain information, and evaluating it on that basis.

DESIGNING AN INFORMATION SYSTEM

The phrase 'information system' sounds rather grand, but it really means no more than taking further the logical argument outlined so far. If we know that we will have to diagnose problems during the coming year, and make decisions, and control our marketing programmes, it makes sense to try to ensure that the information we will need will be available and accessible – that is all an information system means. It may be computerised and highly sophisticated (though this is frankly unlikely outside the largest and wealthiest companies), or it may be simple and paper-based. What is important is the thought that has gone into it.

Following the argument, therefore, we should start by specifying the problems we may have to diagnose, the decisions we may have to make, and the sorts of control information we will need. It is perhaps easier to say what the last may mean than the first two; after all, how do we know what problems will arise, and what decisions we will be called on to make? Experience will guide us to a large extent, since many problems are common, or recur in a similar form. Even if we cannot forecast exactly what will happen, we will probably be able to have a pretty good shot at the broad outline, and that will be better than doing nothing and waiting for the problems to crop up.

Take a manageable portion of your company's operation – say one product or one market – and try the exercise using Worksheet 4.2. Be as specific as possible about the information needed: for example, 'volume and value of sales per product line within each channel by region by month' rather than just 'sales', or 'rating of our brand's major characteristics by consumers aged 25–44 compared with the market leader' rather than just 'consumer acceptance'. At this stage, do not bother too much about where the information will come from; we will discuss that in the next section.

The likely result of such an exercise is a 'wish list' of enormous size: we would love to have information on absolutely everything which might conceivably be relevant. Of course, that is impossible, and would cost more than it would be worth. Just exactly how

WORKSHEET 4.2 INFORMATION NEEDED NEXT YEAR

■ Choose one of the products or markets you know in your firm, and list the *marketing* problems which may occur next year, the decisions you (or the relevant manager) will have to take, and the control measures you would like to check that all is well with the marketing plan. Then try to identify what information would help.

Product/market chosen ....

Information needed

Likely problems

Decisions to be made

Control measures

---

much information it *is* worth having is a complex question, which must be related in the end to the risks involved. If decisions involving many millions of pounds are being made, then the cost of being wrong is high, and money spent on information which helps in the decision is a good investment. Sophisticated mathematical techniques can be used to investigate such questions, but common sense is also helpful.

Other ways of reducing the information to manageable proportions is to ask, for each item listed, two questions:

■ What would I do differently if I had that information?
■ How exactly would I use it?

A former boss of mine with a gift for the telling phrase used to say of some research presented to him that it had a high 'so what' value. Information, however interesting, which produces only the reaction 'so what?' is not worth much.

Types and sources of information

The analysis used in the first three chapters, and the experience of many years, suggest that most companies will need information under the following headings.

Internal
- *Production*
  - production levels, capacity
  - stocks
- *Accounting*
  - costs
  - product profitability
  - customer profitability
  - budgets and reports
- *Sales*
  - orders received
  - sales forecasts
- *Marketing*
  - advertising and promotion spend
  - market research

External
Information on:

- environment
- markets
- competitors
- customers
- consumers
- effects of marketing action

There is of course some overlap between the categories; market research will provide much of the external information, for example, and the accounting budgets and reports will include data on costs and, probably, sales. It is still a useful framework to use as a checklist to prompt questions on what information will come from where.

On internal information, the important point for marketing people is to make sure that they get the information they want in the form that they want it. Information systems run from the centre by computer professionals or accountants may be very efficient, but may ignore the real needs of users. Accounting information in particular is often produced for other purposes, and may be difficult to interpret or, worse, actually misleading.

Evidence in recent years suggests that many standard costing systems, basing allocation of overheads to products on labour costs, may produce seriously misleading results when labour accounts for only a small proportion of total cost (as is quite common nowadays). If overhead allocation is wrong, then the apparent profitability of different products will be wrong, and this may lead to incorrect decisions on resourcing. It is vital that marketing people understand exactly what accounting information can and cannot tell them, and that they make sure that the company information system serves them (not just the other way round).

External sources of information cover a huge range. Apart from formal market research, which is covered briefly in the next section, any company has access to, for example:

- government publications
- international publications (OECD, EU, etc.)
- trade publications (magazines, directories)
- commercial reports
- newspapers and other media
- specialist libraries
- databases

It is the last which has transformed the task of searching for data. A number of computerised databases now exist, some general and some specialised in a particular field; access to the right database can open up huge fields of data. There is of course a cost to any of these sources, and the smaller firm may have to make do with the cheaper ones. Government publications and trade journals, for example, offer a great deal of data, though often the one is somewhat out of date or over-general, while the latter may be subjective and partial.

The last heading in the list – the effects of marketing action –

covers some of the most important and most difficult areas of information. Ideally, as we pointed out earlier, we should like to know what would be the likely effect of any proposed action such as lowering the price or increasing advertising. Such information can be obtained only over time, through careful experimentation and measurement. This is difficult, and can be expensive (though it need not be). It should be the aim to measure effects wherever possible: for example, through putting a coupon in advertisements in different media, or asking callers how they heard of your company; or using different prices in different areas and measuring sales. If effects are never measured, then you will never have more than a very rough idea based on experience. This is often all that you do have, and is a good start; but good, solid information would be better.

In terms of the company's own information system, the point is to try to ensure that:

■ You know what information you want
■ You know what is available from where
■ Someone is responsible for collating it
■ The relevant users know how to access it

The point made earlier is worth repeating: the resulting information system may look simple or sophisticated, may be paper or computer based; what makes the difference to its usefulness is the quality of thinking that has gone into its planning.

Using Worksheet 4.3, try to produce an outline information system for your firm or a part of it, starting from the long list of information in Worksheet 4.2, reduced to a reasonable length, and with possible sources for each piece of information required. You may find it helpful to read the next section on market research first.

MARKET RESEARCH

Market research – or marketing research – is the name given to the range of techniques used to gather information to help marketing analysis, decisions and control. As we have seen, marketing people need a wide array of information from different sources. Much of what we have discussed already could be classified as market

WORKSHEET 4.3 OUTLINE INFORMATION SYSTEM

■ List the *specific* information you think you will need next
    year to help with the marketing of your products/
    services; give exact details, for example 'production
    volume by size and type per week' or 'number of females
    in Hertfordshire between the ages of 18 and 60 who are
    interested in exercise'. Then try to think of where you
    might get that information

	Specific information needed	*Source of information*
Internal		
Production		
Accounting		
Sales		
Marketing		
External		
Environment		
Markets		
Competitors		
Customers		
Consumers		
Effects of marketing action		

research, in particular the secondary sources such as government
publications, databases and so on. This examination of secondary
data (that is, data which have been previously gathered by
someone else for another purpose) should always be the first stage
of any investigation; in Britain it is often referred to as desk
research.

Most of market research activity is devoted to collecting new, or
primary, data. The main sources are:

- experimentation
- observation
- respondents

Although the last-named is commonly thought of as what market research is concerned with, the first two are also fruitful. Experimentation means, as the name suggests, carrying out controlled experiments in the way that scientists do. These experiments can be used in marketing for such things as measuring the effect of different prices, or of different advertising campaigns (as suggested above), or indeed any differences in the marketing programme. There are some questions to which we want answers which only experimentation can provide, since all other methods, such as questionnaire surveys, can measure only proxies. Thus we can question a sample of people about their recall of an advertising campaign, and measure their opinions and attitudes; but if we want to know what the effect is on sales, the only way to do that is by carefully controlled experiment. Such experiments are difficult, but sometimes they are the only way forward.

Observation can also give valuable results. It can range from simply watching people shopping, and seeing what they actually do (sometimes a revealing exercise) to complicated surveys using mechanical methods of recording. For example, most measures of television audiences rely at least partly on meters attached to a sample of TV sets; the meters measure exactly when the set is on and which channel it is tuned to; the results are collected automatically by a central computer. Observation avoids the problem of memory by recording what people actually do. Going back to the issue of understanding the product-in-use, observation of how consumers actually use the product in their own environment is a more accurate method than asking them questions; it deserves to be used more than it is.

The bulk of market research activity, however, is taken up with surveys of some kind. Such surveys can be qualitative or quantitative. Qualitative studies are usually undertaken at the beginning of an investigation, when we do not know much about the topic. Individual depth interviews, or small group discussions, are used to explore the area, to listen to how people talk about the subject, what words they use, what concepts they apply. It can provide very rich data, and furnish hypotheses for further testing. Since only a small number of people can be interviewed using such methods, the results should not be relied on to give a detailed picture of a market; it should always be seen as the first stage of a study.

Quantitative surveys try to put numbers to what we are measuring, and they raise the question as to how we can rely on a survey in which only a few hundred or a few thousand people are sampled from a population of thousands or millions. The answer, which relies for its proof on quite complicated statistical theory, is that we can rely on such samples, provided they are properly constructed, but that surveys give only estimates of the true situation.

The best-known examples of surveys are probably the opinion polls conducted before elections. We are all familiar with the way these are reported, and avidly discussed when they appear to give the 'wrong' answers. In fact, they provide a good example of the extent to which we can rely on survey results. Usually, the two main parties in Britain are quite close in their level of support. What the polls give is an estimate, based on a sample of a certain size, of how people say they intend to vote. Say the results of a particular poll are that 41 per cent favour Party A and 38 per cent Party B. The way we should interpret these figures is that each is subject to a degree of sampling error, and that what we ought to infer is that between say 39 per cent and 43 per cent support A, and between 36 per cent and 40 per cent support B. Clearly, there is an overlap between the two estimates, and it is difficult to conclude firmly that A is in the lead.

Obviously there are a number of other considerations, as there are in a marketing situation. The point is that a survey provides only an estimate, and that it is subject to sampling error; but that, having taken such things into account, we can rely on the results as a basis for our decisions. Generally speaking (and sampling is a complicated business best left to experts), the more precise we want an estimate to be, the larger the sample we have to use. A sample size of less than 100 can give only approximate estimates, and should be treated with caution, though sometimes a little information gathered from even a small sample is better than nothing.

Surveys can be carried out by telephone, by mail, or by personal interview. Telephone interviewing has increased rapidly in Britain in recent years, helped by the wide spread of telephone ownership and by the availability of computer-based systems in which the answers can be input directly into the computer as they are received. Such CATI (computer assisted telephone interviewing) systems can provide extremely fast results, and are relatively cheap; they are obviously limited to subjects which can be asked about over the phone.

Mail surveys are also cheap, but they suffer from the major disadvantage of low response rates (30 per cent is a high response rate for typical mail surveys). They can be useful, but should be treated with care unless some check is made on non-respondents (for example by telephone) to see how they differ from those who have replied.

Personal interviews are the most flexible and reliable source, but they are also the most expensive. The cost can be reduced by adding a few questions to an omnibus survey, many of which are offered by different companies.

There are also many syndicated market research surveys carried out by agencies, which are available on subscription. Such studies cover, for example, panels of retailers and of consumers recording sales or purchases in a wide range of fields. The Market Research Society of Great Britain can supply details of all firms offering research services, and a browse through their year book will show the huge range available. Many of the firms can now also offer research on an international basis.

Most managers will commission and buy research rather than carry it out themselves. They should treat this exactly as they would the buying of any professional service. A clear brief with detailed objectives and as much marketing background as possible will enable the market research experts to offer the best proposals. As with other services, quality is often related to price, and the cheapest quote is not necessarily the most desirable.

5 Using what we can control
The marketing mix, segmentation and targeting

So far we have been looking outside the organisation – at environments and markets, customers, consumers and competitors – which dramatically affect our future but which we cannot control. Now we will turn to what is under our control, to the tools at our disposal in marketing our products and services. This chapter will examine briefly what the main marketing tools are; it will then go on to see how we choose which part of the total market to concentrate on. Later chapters will develop each of the marketing elements separately.

THE MARKETING MIX

The marketing mix is the term given to the tools available to the firm, and to the way it chooses to use them. The best-known way of summarising them was mentioned in Chapter 1: the four Ps. To re-cap, these are:

■ product
■ price
■ promotion
■ place

To be accurate, promotion should be called marketing communications, and place distribution – but four Ps is short and memorable, and a useful shorthand. People have argued that it is too short. We saw in Chapter 1 that in services marketing it is suggested that a further three Ps are needed (people, process and physical evidence), and there are other formulations put forward by writers. The four Ps has stood the test of time, however, and will be used here, accepting that it is a simplification. Let us look briefly at each element of the mix.

Product

By product we mean the total offering the firm makes to the market. As we made clear in Chapter 1, most firms offer a combination of physical product and services, and a broad view of the firm's offering is the best from a marketing perspective. Naturally, we should stress that it is the customer's and consumer's view of our offering that is important.

The firm's product or service is central to its existence, and must be regarded as the most important element in the mix. It can be broken down into:

- physical attributes
- psychological attributes
- quality
- styling, features
- branding, including name
- packaging
- assortment (sizes, varieties, colours etc.)
- range and line
- services
- guarantee, warranty and returns policy

(adapted from Randall 1993)

- *Price*: This is self-explanatory, though marketing people will often take a different view of pricing from, say, accountants. From the marketing viewpoint, price is very much a part of the marketing mix, and gives the buyer important signals about the quality and positioning of the brand.
- *Promotion*: As mentioned earlier, this should really be called communications, as it covers all the means the firm uses to communicate with the market. This includes advertising, sales promotion, personal selling and all other forms of publicity.
- *Place*: Most products need some form of channel of distribution; some are simple, others complex. This element has been neglected in many marketing fields, but has become increasingly important as retailer power has grown. In some fields, it has become perhaps

the single most important determinant of brand success after the product itself.

These then are the weapons at our disposal. Marketing people would claim to have at least an influence on all of them, and a decisive one on some. In fact, as we saw in Chapter 1, this can lead to conflict with other functions in the firm. In many companies, for example, marketing does not have a great deal of influence over the product; in others, over the price. But both are essential elements of the way the firm and its products are seen by customers and consumers. If marketing is to have any real impact on the firm's future, it must have some say in every element of the mix.

Clearly, different firms use the marketing mix in very different ways. A heavy engineering firm will invest large amounts in the product, in ensuring the highest quality and technical standards; it will probably have highly trained technical sales people, but it will spend little or nothing on advertising. Firms such as Procter & Gamble or Unilever, on the other hand, who between them make many of the household brands we use, spend a great deal on advertising and promotion and (these days anyway) comparatively little on the sales force. This does not of course mean that they do not invest in product quality and manufacturing, because they do; it is simply the balance that is different. Many services firms spend a great deal on the people aspect of their product, through training for example; some spend heavily on advertising while others rely on word of mouth. The marketing task is to develop the most appropriate mix to match the firm with its markets and competitors.

Using Worksheet 5.1, try to analyse the marketing mix adopted by different firms. You do not need to be totally accurate, but to develop an overall picture. Look at the products and their advertising, distribution and pricing to see how your impressions are borne out by the facts. Then try to describe your own employer's marketing mix, either for the firm as a whole, or for a distinct part of it; use real figures here if you can.

SEGMENTATION

Before going on to discuss how the firm should best match its mix to the marketplace, we must spend a little time going back to that marketplace and the firm's relation to it. We have rather assumed

WORKSHEET 5.1 DESCRIBING THE MARKETING MIX

■ For each company/product, rank the apparent importance of the elements of the mix, and give some comment
or description. Apply the technique to your own firm, or
a part of it.

■ Within the Product section, choose the three most
important aspects from the list on page 60 (physical
attributes, psychological attributes etc.). For example,
you might say that for Ford cars, price is ranked first,
physical product attributes second, promotion third and
distribution fourth; or you might think some other
ranking is more appropriate. For Timotei, psychological
attributes first, and so on.

	Ford cars	*Timotei shampoo*	*Amstrad computers*	*Your firm*
Product				
Rank				
Comment				
Price				
Rank				
Comment				
Promotion				
Rank				
Comment				
Place				
Rank				
Comment				

that the market was one undifferentiated whole, with all firms competing in all of it. That is not true; different competitors often aim at different parts of the market.

In many markets, there are groups of people with different needs and wants. These groups, called segments in the marketing jargon, should ideally be very like each other *within* the groups and very unlike each other *between* groups; firms can then design products for each group separately. Thus, for example, in the toothpaste market, there may be one group who like only peppermint flavour and another who like only spearmint.

The first task for marketing is therefore to discover whether segments exist or not in their particular market, and what size they are. In some markets, this is relatively simple and straightforward, but in others it is not. This is particularly so in mature markets in which manufacturers have spent time and money searching out and developing segments, trying to differentiate their product offerings from their competitors. In such markets, the technology may be fairly mature and the products may be physically similar to each other. The manufacturers may offer more and more slightly different models to appeal to groups of consumers with slightly different needs. Sometimes, the manufacturers may lead the market to the extent that consumers in expressing their needs and wants in market research are just playing back what the manufacturers have been telling them.

In a very fragmented market such as shampoo, there are hundreds of brands, all of which wash the hair fairly efficiently but all of which claim to offer something slightly different. There are some clear, large segments – medicated, anti-dandruff, beauty – but beyond that it is difficult to determine what real segments exist and what merely reflects manufacturers' actions.

The situation is confused by the fact that in most markets, both consumer and industrial, most buyers buy several brands with differing frequencies. It is therefore inaccurate to perceive most markets as being made up of people who only ever buy one brand (and therefore belong unambiguously to one segment). In your own experience, you probably use different restaurants and cafes at different times for example, and therefore you form part of different segments; but you probably use only one bank at any one period, so it is important to look at the specific market you are concerned with.

Using your observation, try to find out what segments exist in a market you know or have access to. This might involve looking at brands in a supermarket or high street store, examining advertisements, talking to buyers and users, or using data you have access to. Concentrate on trying to understand the benefits buyers are looking for, rather than only on obvious differences such as price (though price may be an important discriminator in your market). Summarise your findings in Worksheet 5.2, and go on to describe the segments in your firm's market, again in terms of the benefits different groups are looking for.

In order to go from the pattern of segmentation to some decisions on the marketing mix, we have to start to describe the

WORKSHEET 5.2 BENEFIT SEGMENTS

■ Choose a market you know, have access to, or can study. Split it into a small number of segments (say three to five) and describe what benefits the people in each segment are looking for. For example, a fast food segment, in which the products bought are McDonald's, Wimpy, Kentucky Fried Chicken etc.; the benefits would be speed, convenience, low price and so on.

Market chosen ....

	Segment	*Products/ brands bought*	*Description of benefits sought by buyers in this segment*
1			
2			
3			
4			
5			

actual people in the segments so that we can target them. Most segmentation exercises therefore set out to find groups of people with similar buying habits. They use one or more of a number of bases for segmentation in consumer markets:

- demographic
- socio-economic
- geo-demographic
- buying patterns
- personality, attitudes, values
- life style

The rule generally is to start with the simple, easy-to-measure base and go on to more complex ones only if necessary.

Demographic measures are age, sex, region, family size, family composition, life-cycle stage. Some markets are clearly segmented by age and sex, though it is important to make sure that one's expectations are actually true (70 per cent of disposable razors are bought by women, for example). Family size and composition are changing fairly rapidly, and the old image of the typical family of two adults and around two children no longer reflects reality. Such changes of course may offer new opportunities for segmented products, as well as threats to old ones.

Socio-economic measures refer both to wealth and income, and to social class. The former have also changed rapidly in recent years; some observers see the development of a split market, with a large economy sector occupied by people with little money, and a premium sector occupied by the smaller number with large incomes. Such changes have to be monitored with care. Social class is of declining importance in most markets, though marketing people in Britain seem strangely attached to it. The old analysis often turns up in discussion and is indeed used in marketing decisions, though it has surely outlived its usefulness. For the record, the common classification is based on the occupation of the head of household (itself becoming an outdated concept), and gives the following groups:

AB: upper middle class, top managers and professionals
C1: junior managers and professionals, white-collar workers
C2: skilled manual workers

D: unskilled manual workers
E: those living at the lowest levels of subsistence

A much more useful measure is the geo-demographic, which might be regarded as a combination of the previous two. It is based on housing type, classified by postcode into tight types of neighbourhood. The broad classification of the best known, ACORN (a classification of residential neighbourhoods), is:

A: agricultural areas
B: modern family housing, higher incomes
C: older housing of intermediate status
D: poor quality older terraced housing
E: better-off council estates
F: less well-off council estates
G: poorest council estates
H: multi-racial areas
I: high status non-family areas
J: affluent suburban housing
K: better-off retirement areas

Buying patterns can be useful, though as already mentioned most people buy a repertoire of brands, and classifying them into distinct groups may not be easy. The terms heavy buyers/light buyers/non-buyers are often used and can again be useful as long as the assumptions about why people fall into these groups is questioned. For example, are these people non-buyers because the manufacturers have not offered them a product they want, or because the distribution does not reach them, and so on.

The fields of personality, attitudes, values and life style have seen some highly publicised studies, and a great deal of hype. Such studies are usually called on when the more straighforward methods produce little of value. It is tempting to think that, because some brands have distinct personalities which consumers are quite capable of describing, then they must appeal to buyers with different personalities. There are groups of people who seem to behave in similar ways, including which products and brands they buy. Unfortunately, no method has proved to be generally successful over time in different markets. As many of the segmentation studies in this field use rather complex statistical methods, potential users are advised to approach them carefully and with some scepticism (though not necessarily cynicism).

Industrial markets are often simpler to segment than consumer ones, but not always. There are equivalents to demographics in terms of industry, company size and region; and for buying patterns, for example. As the earlier discussion on organisational buying suggested, buyers in industry are human too, and it is possible that some of the personality/attitude approaches could be used. It is much more likely that harder measures based on needs and buying processes will be fruitful, however.

Using Worksheet 5.3 try segmenting some more markets, this time describing the people in each segment. Apply any of the segmentation bases described above, or ones you develop yourself. Then do the same for your own firm.

WHAT TO DO WITH SEGMENTATION

Assuming that segments exist, what should you do about them? There are five decision stages:

1 Evaluate the segments
2 Choose a segmentation strategy
3 Select the segments to be targeted
4 Develop a targeted marketing mix for each
5 Allocate resources to the segments

Evaluation means deciding what the segment is worth to you: is it big enough to be worthwhile, can you reach it, does it suit your firm? A segment which a large multi-national decides is not worth bothering with may be of great interest to a small local firm.

The strategies available are usually described as undifferentiated, differentiated and concentrated (Kotler 1991).

An undifferentiated strategy means offering the same product to the whole market, as Coca-Cola used to do, or Henry Ford did with his Model T ('Any color you like as long as it's black'). In the early stages of a market, this strategy may offer the biggest rewards, especially if there are substantial economies of scale available.

A differentiated strategy therefore means offering different products to the different segments. Most car manufacturers now

WORKSHEET 5.3 PEOPLE IN SEGMENTS

- ■ Again, use information you have or can get, or just guess.
- ■ Try to identify the sort of people you would find in each segment of the markets shown, and in your own market(s). In recorded music, you might suggest segments such as top twenty, heavy metal, light classical, authentic baroque music, and so on.

Product field	*Products/brands*	*Description of buyers/users*
Recorded music		
Segment		
1		
2		
3		
Insurance		
Segment		
1		
2		
3		
Transport		
Segment		
1		
2		
3		
Your company		
Segment		
1		
2		
3		

do this, although few cover the whole market. A differentiated strategy may deliver higher total sales than an undifferentiated one, though costs may be higher and there is always the danger of cannibalisation (eating your own sales and profits).

Concentrated marketing focuses only on a part of the total market, as Dunhill or Mercedes do. The part may be large or small, though the assumption is that it is small relative to the market as a whole.

Which strategy you adopt is to some extent a matter of overall corporate strategy, not just marketing, but clearly marketing ought to have an important influence. Your freedom of action will depend to a great extent on your history and current position, and on your strengths and weaknesses in relation to the nature of the market and your competitors.

Selecting the segments in which to operate is also a matter of matching your strengths and weaknesses to the opportunities and threats confronting you. A large, well-funded company has more choices than a small firm with limited finances; but the small firm may be more flexible, better able to take advantage of developing segments and small niches.

TARGETING THE MARKETING MIX

We can now return to the mix, and try to decide how to target it on each of our chosen segments. The basic process of matching the firm to its market and its competitors is seen here at its clearest. How exactly do we compete in this segment? How do we make the most of our resources, given what the segment wants and what competitors are doing?

Since we have to start from where we are, some of the decisions are probably already taken. The overall pattern of the mix is probably heavily influenced by history: 'That's the way we have always done it.' Anyone reading this book will regard this as a position at least worth challenging. Experience and conventional wisdom have a lot to offer, and the conventional way of doing things may be the best – but it may not.

The fundamental marketing approach must be applied. The questions to be asked are:

■ Who are the buyers (and users etc.) in this segment?

- What are their needs and wants?
- Where does our product fit in (the product-in-use)?
- How do they decide on what to buy?
- What influences their decision?
- How can I influence that decision, and at what stages?
- Which element of the mix will make the greatest impact?
- How should I balance the different elements of the mix?

The answers to some of these questions are of course extremely difficult to find. Nevertheless, decisions should take them into account, explicitly, even if deduction and guesswork play a major part.

There are two further sets of considerations which will affect the mix adopted. The first is the all too common one that the resources available will not be enough; the second is how one makes general judgements as to the appropriateness of the mix.

As to the first, it leads straight back to the basic problem of knowing the effect of marketing action. If we knew exactly how the market and our competitors would react to a given marketing action by us, we could optimise the mix. We would allocate money to the element which produced the best return, then when that was used up we would allocate to the next best return, and so on. So in a particular situation, if advertising promised the best return we would allocate funds to the advertising budget until diminishing returns set in; at this point an improvement in product quality offers the best return on investment, so we allocate funds to that; and so on.

Unfortunately, we do not have the models to provide such information in most cases. The basic approach is, however, worth considering. That is, after all, what we are doing implicitly when we allocate money to the different elements of the mix. Surely it is better to make the process explicit, so that we can have serious discussion about the decisions, and perhaps start to measure effects and learn more about improving our decision-making.

As to the second, more general question, we can apply some basic tests. Every marketing mix should:

- Be coherent, with all the elements giving the same message and pulling in the same direction
- Use the most effective combination of the elements in the given situation

WORKSHEET 5.4 EVALUATION OF THE MARKETING MIX

■ Take a part of your firm (or the whole if it is appropriate) and describe a particular segment and the
marketing mix targeted at it. Evaluate the mix, awarding
marks out of ten for each criterion. Summarise any
corrective action you think necessary as a result of the
exercise.

Description of segment

1 Your products bought:
2 Benefits sought:
3 Description of buyers:

Description of marketing mix

Product:
Price (in relation to competitors):
Promotion (amount and type):
Place:

Evaluation of mix   *Marks*

Coherence
Effectiveness
Match to segment characteristics and needs
Fit with company history
Builds on strengths, minimises weaknesses
Differentiates from competitors

Summary of corrective action needed

■ Match the target segment's characteristics and needs
■ Be consistent with the brand's history
■ Fit the company's history and culture
■ Build on the company's strengths and minimise its weaknesses
■ Differentiate the company and its products from competitors.

Now try to evaluate your company's marketing mix using Work-sheet 5.4. If corrective action is needed, how would you go about trying to achieve it?

6 *Existing products, new products*

Deciding what we should be offering our customers

We have already noted that the product is at the heart of the firm, indeed perhaps *is* the firm. In these circumstances, marketing cannot claim sole rights to decisions about what products and services are offered. Manufacturing or operations, for example, will have a powerful voice, and the history and culture of the company will frequently be determining factors.

Nonetheless, given the fundamental importance of making what customers and consumers want, rather than what the firm thinks it is good at, marketing must have a significant influence on product decisions. In many firms, this is not so, and marketing is still seen as something done after the product has been designed and manufactured. It cannot be stresed often enough that this is a short-sighted and misconceived view, and that marketing must contribute to policies concerned with what products are offered in what form to whom.

This chapter, then, will take a marketing view of product policy, looking first at how we can evaluate our current range, then at decisions concerning existing products, and finally at the development of new products.

PORTFOLIO ANALYSIS

The first step, as always, must be to understand where we are now: what is the state of health of our current range of products, or product portfolio? Most firms have more than one product, some have scores, or hundreds or even thousands. The more products there are, the more likely it is that they are grouped in some way, either by technology or manufacturing, or by customer industry, or by region or by some combination of these. Let us assume that we are looking at a manageable range of products for a company or subsidiary (though top management must of course look at all the products at once). How do we make sense of what may be a complex and confusing picture?

A very early stage must be to look at sales and profitability, as was suggested in an earlier chapter. This information is fundamental. In some industries, where there are very many products, and large common costs, it is difficult to attribute profitability very precisely to individual products, and in those cases it must be done by product group. Some overall view must be taken, however, of where sales and profits are being made. (The caution offered earlier as to the reliability of some accounting data is repeated here: make absolutely sure that you understand what the accountants' figures are really saying, and what assumptions underly them.)

Current sales and profits are an essential starting point, but they are not the only view required. In particular, we need to look forward, to where we shall be making sales and profits in future. An early framework for doing this was offered by Peter Drucker, one of the few authentic management gurus. His recommendation, made in the 1960s, is still valid; he said that you should divide the firm's products into the following categories:

- *Today's breadwinners*: substantial volume, adequate contribution, at or near their zenith
- *Tomorrow's breadwinners*: show promise and reality, consumer and trade acceptance, high contribution
- *Productive specialities*: having a limited and distinct market
- *Development products*: future as yet uncertain
- *Failures*: all firms have some
- *Yesterday's breadwinners*: still high volume, but low net revenue
- *Repair jobs*: must have all the following characteristics:
  - substantial volume
  - considerable growth opportunities
  - a significant leadership position
  - high probability of exceptional results if successful
  - one major defect only
- *Unnecessary or unjustified specialities*: returns not justified given costs and management time

■ *Investments in managerial ego*: products in which senior management reputations are involved
■ *Cinderellas*: sleepers who may one day awake

This categorisation is to some extent qualitative, but it is a
powerful one. Most managers will recognise many of the product
types described, without going further (are there any investments
in managerial ego in your firm?).

Using the data you gathered for Chapter 3, and any other
knowledge you can find, put your firm's products into Drucker's
categories, using Worksheet 6.1.

Drucker's argument is that, if the firm's continued existence
today is guaranteed by today's breadwinners, then its future
depends on tomorrow's breadwinners. Management time and
effort must be spent on these, not frittered away on products which
will never produce the sales and profits needed. Too often,
because of managers' careers, or internal politics, or the company's
history, far too much time is given to yesterday's breadwinners or
repair jobs or unjustified specialities. It must be said, of course,
that the judgement as to what constitutes a Cinderella as opposed
to an investment in managerial ego is a difficult one at the time.
Only with hindsight do we all have twenty-twenty vision, and
sometimes a stubborn manager can continue with what seems to
everyone else a hopeless case, only to see it triumph in the end.
There are examples of such products – the Xerox plain paper
copier, for instance, or the computer disk drive – but they are few
and far between.

Applying Drucker's thinking to your own firm, how well allo-
cated is management time and effort to your various products?

In the last twenty years, there have been more sophisticated
models offered to help in the task of evaluating the portfolio. Some
have become famous, such as the Boston matrix, which divided
products up according to market share and market growth rate.
The quadrants into which products fall were imaginatively named
cash cows, stars, question marks and dogs. These bear a remark-
able similarity to some of Drucker's categories. Although the
model has an attractive simplicity, it is also subject to some severe
criticisms. Like all similar models (and there are several described
in textbooks), it can appear to provide concrete answers which are
not justified by the assumptions made and the nature of the

WORKSHEET 6.1 DRUCKER'S CATEGORIES

■ Put your company's products (or those of your division or area) into the categories suggested by Drucker. Put the sales and/or profit of each (from previous worksheets) and draw conclusions about the future.

Category	*Products*	*Sales or %*	*Profits or %*
Today's breadwinners			
Tomorrow's breadwinners			
Productive specialities			
Development products			
Failures			
Yesterday's breadwinners			
Repair jobs			
Unnecessary/ unjustified specialities			
Investments in managerial ego			
Cinderellas			

analysis. At this stage, you are recommended to stick to simpler approaches such as Drucker's.

MANAGING THE PRODUCT MIX AND PRODUCT LINES

The product mix refers to the number of different product fields the firm operates in. Some companies such as the American General Electric are in many very different markets and have a broad product mix: aircraft engines, broadcasting, defence electronics, factory automation, electric lighting, domestic appliances and many others in that case. Nestlé, on the other hand, although it has many thousands of products worldwide, is mainly in one industry – food – and is therefore said to have a narrow product mix.

The breadth of a firm's product mix has a lot to do with its history, and with current trends in management. The previous fashion for diversification seems to have run its course, and the present trend is towards concentrating on markets and products one knows well ('Sticking to the knitting'). Marketing has little specific to offer in determining what is the right product mix for a particular company, except its analysis of where markets are going and what products will be needed to succeed in them. In Worksheet 6.2, describe your firm's product mix, and try to say in what direction it is going. If it is moving in a particular direction, is that because of a thought-out strategy, or is it accidental? Does it reflect a good match between the way markets are moving and your company's strengths and weaknesses?

The product line refers to the number of products offered within a particular field or market; a product line is said to be deep if it contains a relatively large number of products, versions, models etc. Again, the depth of a firm's line is likely to be the result of its history and the way its markets have developed. As a generalisation, larger firms will tend to have deeper lines than small firms (though not always, as Coca-Cola and Guinness showed for much of their history). What should be done about it is discussed in the later section on modification, addition and deletion.

WORKSHEET 6.2 THE PRODUCT MIX

■ List the number of separate markets and product lines your firm is involved in. Broadly, different technology or production facilities mean a separate product line; different selling and distribution channels mean different markets. For example, a financial services company may have insurance, unit trust and portfolio management products; each may have one or more markets, such as private investors, companies and pension funds.

■ Compare the situation today with that of 5 years ago, and with what you expect to be true 5 years from now to gauge the trend (tick in the 5 years ago and future columns).

Product lines   Markets (now)   5 years ago   Future

Conclusion: product mix is:

Broad _____ *Narrow*

Trend is towards:

ALLOCATING RESOURCES TO PRODUCTS

One of the major decisions to be made in product policy is how to allocate resources between the various lines and individual products. This is where the various models mentioned earlier are supposed to help, but they have their limitations. They can also be dangerous, as there have been many cases in which products or divisions identified as cash cows have been starved of cash so that other products can be supported; in fact, the products responsible for today's sales and profits also need investment if they are not to be irretrievably weakened.

Drucker's approach is also designed to guide such decisions, though implicitly rather than explicitly: effort and resources should be put into tomorrow's breadwinners, for example, but only limited amounts into repair jobs and unnecessary specialities.

These are difficult and complicated decisions, since the scarce resources – cash and quality management time – will always be limited. Marketing's contribution should be on the markets and the way they are moving, ensuring that the company's products make the most of current strengths and are ready to take advantage of developing opportunities. Frequently, marketing will also be arguing for investment which will not show an immediate return: sacrificing short-term profit for a consolidation of brand share, for example. Since this is a perennial argument, it is worth spending a little time on the idea of market share.

The importance of market share

In recent years, evidence from a number of sources has underlined the importance of a firm's or product's share of its market in determining profitability. Some of these findings are summarised here.

■ Market share is the most important determinant of profitability across a range of industries.

■ Brands with a market share of 40 per cent generate three times the return of those with a share of only 10 per cent.

■ For UK grocery brands, the number one brand generates over six times the return on sales of the number two brand, while the number three and four brands are unprofitable.

■ For US consumer goods, the number one brand earned a 20 per cent return, the number two earned around 5 per cent and the rest lost money.

These findings, and in consumer markets the increasing power of retailers, has meant that market share has become a dominant strategic aim for many firms. Some, such as the French company BSN, have declared that they will compete only in markets in which they can be number one or two (on a European or world basis).

There are, of course, alternative strategies, in particular the search for a profitable niche. A strong brand in a niche market can earn a higher return than a brand leader in a large mass market, because in the latter case the potential profits are competed away by the big companies slugging it out for dominance.

This underlines, too, the importance of the correct definition of the market you serve; changing the definition of your market will change your market share, and may alter your conclusions about the future. Ideally, product policy should aim to build dominant shares of each served market or segment.

That may, to return to the earlier argument, involve a short-term sacrifice of profit. We are familiar with the allegation that the British and Americans are driven by stock market pressures to short termism in strategic decisions, while the Japanese and Germans take a longer-term view and so can build dominant shares over a period. It may therefore be time for marketing people to take a role in arguing their strategy to their board and to the City, in that investment in a strong brand position may take just as long to show a return as investment in research and development or in a new plant. The theme of the value of brands is covered in a later section of this chapter.

In Worksheet 6.3, compare your market shares and profitability. This is a similar exercise to that of Worksheet 3.3, and once again, you should look for patterns and surprises. Do your results bear out the generalisations set out above? If not, what is the explanation?

MODIFICATION, ADDITION AND DELETION OF PRODUCTS

Product lines rarely stay still, since the world is always moving on. Individual products, and the line as a whole, need to be constantly reviewed and changed.

The pressure for modification can come either from marketing, or from elsewhere in the company. If from marketing, it should be an attempt to improve the product in terms of its performance for customers and consumers, or to differentiate it from competitors' products. As the product is the heart of the firm, so quality is the heart of the product. Marketing's role is to ensure that quality is firmly anchored in what its buyers and users want, and that as far as possible that quality can be differentiated from competitors'.

WORKSHEET 6.3 MARKET SHARE AND PROFITABILITY

■ Using the data from exercises in Chapter 3, take the major products (accounting for a majority of your sales and profits) and compare their market share and profitability. Give (or estimate) the share each holds of its served market, i.e. the market in which it mainly competes; this might be a part of a bigger market, for example, crisps rather than the whole snack market. Use a measure such as profit as a percentage of sales, and actual profit.

Product	Market share	Profitability	Actual profit	% of total

This theme, again, is returned to in the later discussion of branding.

This search for improvement should be permanent. One of the things which really does seem to distinguish the best Japanese companies from many of their western competitors is that they are constantly looking to improve a product from the moment it is launched, whereas some western firms seem to heave a sigh of relief and think they have breathing space before they need to think again. Modifications have a cost, and that needs to be set against future profits; but experience suggests that it is well worth incurring some extra cost in order to gain some real consumer advantage, especially one which differentiates against competition.

Other pressures for modification from within will come either from manufacturing or from general cost pressures. The manufacturing department will want to make changes for the sake of efficiency or easier production, and quite rightly so. What marketing must do is to make sure that any such change does not detract from the performance of the product-in-use. Procter &

Gamble were reputed to call their marketing people 'the house-wife's representative in the company', which is a neat way of putting this point of view.

One of the difficulties of tracking changes is that if they are frequent, any single one may make little or no perceptible difference – but over time the quality can decline. Only constant checking against known standards can avoid this.

Take three recent modifications made in your firm's products, and in Worksheet 6.4 summarise where the impetus for change came from, whether marketing was involved, and any comments on the outcome.

ADDITION

Additions to a product line are common. They often come from stretching or filling the line, self-explanatory terms for similar

WORKSHEET 6.4 PRODUCT MODIFICATIONS

■ Identify three modifications which have been made to your products in the last few years, and try to analyse how they came about.

Product	Modification	Suggested by (dept)	Checked by mktg?	Comment on result

■ What conclusions can you draw about the process of product modification in your company?

activities. Such additions can be offensive, that is, designed to capture a new or developing segment; or defensive, that is, to block competitors' possible moves.

Line extensions, as these are called, are the easiest way to launch additional products, since they normally build on the name and goodwill of existing brands, and there is clearly an argument for capitalising on past success. There is a counter-argument, that too much reliance on extension will tend to weaken the parent brand. That is clearly true when the addition is a failure which may reflect on the reputation of the parent, but some critics go further and say that *any* extension of a strong brand is dangerous.

Since there are examples of strong brands which have remained more or less un-extended, and brands which have developed whole families successfully, there is no firm conclusion possible on this question. Each individual situation must be reviewed carefully. If an extension fills a real customer/consumer need, and is of comparable quality with its parent, then it should be allowed to go ahead. What should be avoided is 'me-too' products which simply ape competition and offer nothing different to buyers; the only excuse for such additions is if they make a serious dent in competitors' sales and profits, but that is more often a hope than a reality.

DELETION

Deleting products seems to be an emotionally taxing issue, especially when they are products which the firm has made for a long time, and even more if they are the products on which the company was founded. Even so, most products eventually outlive their usefulness; if they are taking up valuable resources and management time, they must be pruned.

This is not necessarily a straightforward decision, if the product under threat is part of a line which customers or consumers are used to. If being part of a line is in itself of value – for example if the wholesaler or retailer wants to carry a full line – then pruning an old product may not make sense as long as it is making some positive contribution.

Another check which should be made is whether the product could be revived. Many old-established products have been neglected for years, and may have received little quality management attention. Sometimes, imagination and some investment may revive them.

■ Ribena was an old-established (some would say old-fashioned) brand of blackcurrant drink given to young children as a dietary supplement. Times had changed and diets improved; Ribena sales were declining, and it may have been a candidate for eventual deletion. However, a new version was launched, ready-to-drink in small cartons. This answered the changes in the marketplace, appealed directly to children of a much wider age range, and was very successful in its own right. Not only that, it revived the sales of the parent brand.

Often, however, a product has merely sentimental value and is contributing nothing. Following the checks outlined, including asking customers and consumers for their reaction, deletion should release resources which can be better employed on products which will ensure the firm's future.

Review your own product lines, and in Worksheet 6.5 list some candidates for modification, addition and deletion, giving your

WORKSHEET 6.5 CHANGES TO THE PRODUCT LINE

■ Taking the major components of your product mix, as before, review the total and make recommendations as to modifications, additions and deletions. Give reasons for each, and then try to guess how acceptable each recommendation would be to top management.

Product	Modification, addition, deletion	Reasoning	Acceptability to management Why? Why not?

reasoning. Could this convince your top management to agree to your recommendations?

BRANDING

A brand is more than a product; it has associations and values in buyers' minds which distinguish it from competing products; frequently, users are prepared to pay more for a brand, or to search it out. Brands are usually associated with consumer markets: Mars, Guinness, Persil. However, there are strong brands in business markets too: British Airways, IBM (until recently), JCB. Services can be branded, too: apart from airlines, think of McDonald's, or the Forte hotel ranges (Forte Crest, Forte TrustHouse etc.).

The examples quoted earlier on market share were mainly based on brands, and there is no doubt that a strong brand is potentially very profitable. It takes time and money to build up, and if properly managed will have a long life; the same brands have been leaders of their category for over thirty years, sometimes longer (think of Hovis, Kellogg's Cornflakes, Gillette razors, and so on). It is for this reason that in recent years some spectacular prices have been paid in take-overs of companies with strong brands (Rowntree, Nabisco, for example).

Some people, particularly from outside marketing, are prone to talk about brand image, and 'improving the image', as if this were something superficial and easy to do. In fact, although a strong brand does have an image, often a powerful one, it is something which is not accidental. There are functional and non-functional elements of a brand: it must perform its task effectively, and it may have additional values which are symbolic or value-expressive. It is of course important to communicate these values to buyers, and it is here that it helps to think about the image.

■ The major success of a strong brand, however, comes back to its fundamental quality as a product-in-use. Customers and consumers are well able to tell what works and what does not in practice; they will choose what works best and gives value for money.

All the firm's efforts, therefore – R&D, manufacturing, marketing

– must be devoted to finding and developing ways in which the brand can deliver this quality in a way which separates it from competition.

A brand has four main functions for buyers:

- *Identity*: the brand must identify itself through its name and design
- *Shorthand summary*: the identity should act as a summary of all the information held about it
- *Security*: a familiar brand should be reassuring, as the quality expected should be guaranteed
- *Added value*: in some way, and mainly in fundamental quality as a product-in-use, the brand must offer more than the generic product

There are always threats to brands, either from outside in the form of competitors, or from inside in the form of short-term pressures discussed earlier, or neglect, or sheer greed. Many commentators recently have suggested that there is a swing away from brands in the hearts and minds of consumers. Evidence of this is the dramatic price reductions made by Philip Morris in the USA for its cigarette brands, in reaction to the huge inroads made by discount products. It is possible to argue, on the other hand, that this case merely demonstrates that management greed (they had increased the price of Marlboro by 10 per cent a year for many years) can be self-defeating; in the end, consumers showed that they were not being offered added value by Marlboro to the extent that its premium price demanded.

It is too early to say whether the 1990s will show a real change in consumer preferences from the brand-addicted 1980s. The soundest argument seems to be that brands which genuinely meet consumers' needs with superior and differentiating quality will continue to win sales, premium prices and profits – but that, as always, they must offer perceived value for money.

In building and maintaining brands, the critical success factors are five:

1   *Quality*: as has been stressed constantly, this is fundamental.
2   *Differentiation*: has again been stressed throughout.
3   *Consistency*: is the hallmark of great brands such as Persil or

Mars; frequent change will only confuse buyers; this does not mean standing absolutely still.

4 *Evolution*: is essential to keep up with changing markets and needs; Fairy Liquid has been consistent in claiming and delivering quality, but has changed its platform steadily over the years.

5 *Support*: in consumer brands, this means consistent, heavy advertising support; for business brands it may mean heavy R&D or highly trained sales people giving extensive consultancy support; for services it may mean real commitment to staff training; re-investment of profits is essential.

NEW PRODUCT DEVELOPMENT

The development of new products is essential for most firms, since existing products will have a limited life: competition, changing needs and technological developments are major threats. Beyond this, many company plans demand more growth than the existing products can deliver. Unfortunately, although many firms claim to be committed to new product development (NPD), few have a very good track record in launching successful new brands.

The failure rate for new products is variously quoted as between 50 per cent and 90 per cent (depending on definitions of new products, launch and failure). Whatever the rate, it is very high, and the majority of funds devoted to NPD are spent on projects which do not succeed.

Many of the reasons for new product failure are organisational, in that many if not most firms are in practice hostile to innovation. Whatever they say, they put barriers in the way of new ideas; bureaucracy and entrenched interests block new ways of doing things.

From a marketing viewpoint, there are plenty of things which can go wrong.

One list of reasons for failure gives these:

1 Lack of meaningful product uniqueness
2 Poor price-value performance
   - three out of four successful products were better than competitors in some way
   - four out of five failures were the same as or worse than competitors

3   Poor planning (including segmentation, budgeting, market understanding, poor research, over-enthusiasm)
4   Wrong timing
5   Action by competitors
6   Product performance
7   Lack of a product champion/internal politics

Many of the ideas put forward in this and earlier chapters are echoed here. What distinguishes successful firms from the less successful is often that the good company actually practises what it professes. Many people know what is the right thing to do, but few actually do it – consistently.

In examining successful innovation, one is forced to the conclusion that it is often a chaotic process. Innovation is by definition disruptive, and firms which are good at it seem somehow to be able to tolerate people and processes which go against the normal rules. Often, for example, new products are developed by a group outside the normal organisational framework, left to themselves with comparatively few resources but equally few constraints.

Insofar as it is possible to state general rules, it appears that successful new products are geared to market needs, and that they are developed by a team which crosses or ignores organisation boundaries, led by a product champion – someone who possesses strong leadership qualities, has both technical and marketing skills, and can over-ride disappointment and temporary failure.

It follows that it is difficult to recommend firm procedures which, if followed, will lead to success. The models which exist usually show a series of stages through which a new product will pass.

1   idea generation
2   screening
3   physical development
4   communications development
5   market testing
6   final checks
7   launch

In reality, a project may pass through several of these simultaneously, or miss one out; it will almost certainly circle back

WORKSHEET 6.6 NEW PRODUCT DEVELOPMENT RATING

■ Compare your firm with the competitor which seems most successful at new product development, and give yourself a rating out of 10 for overall success, speed and each stage of the process. Then take two examples of NPD in your firm in the last few years, one success and one failure, and try to analyse the reasons, using the list given in the chapter (and adding your own). What conclusions can you draw for improving your record?

Rating for overall success at launching new products:

Rating for speed at launching new products:

Ratings for each stage:
   Idea generation   ...
   Screening   ...
   Physical development   ...
   Communications development ...
   Market testing   ...
   Final checks   ...
   Launch   ...

Successful new product   *Failure*

■ Describe the process and result.

Conclusions about improvements to process

through some more than once. The framework is useful, however, in setting up a series of checks or hurdles through which each project must pass; senior management should be involved at these stages in a thorough and objective review.

The marketing viewpoint ought to be represented throughout, since without market acceptability brilliance in any other aspect is useless. Marketing people are sometimes accused, on the other hand, of resisting real technical innovation, preferring instead an imitation of what already exists. The more original the innovation, the more difficult it is to judge the market acceptability; sometimes, it is up to management flair and judgement to take the risk and back a hunch.

In looking at your own firm, the first question to ask is whether it has a new product strategy or not. Is there clear commitment to a new product development policy, and how does it manifest itself? Is it mere words, or is there a commitment of resources and a toleration of the time and effort taken to follow leads, sometimes down blind alleys? Does it try to be a leader in its markets, or a follower? How is the process carried out? How could it be improved?

Worksheet 6.6 gives you the opportunity to try out some of these judgements, and asks you to analyse two new product projects that have taken place – one successful, one unsuccessful. Can you draw any lessons from this for the future?

7 Setting the price
Satisfying marketing and profit objectives

If the product and the brand discussed in the previous chapter are at the heart of the company and must therefore take pride of place in the marketing mix, then price must rank second in importance. All business is about buying and selling, and the price at which you buy and sell is a major determinant of profit and loss. No other element of the mix has such a direct and sometimes dramatic effect on the bottom line.

An example will make this clearer. In Table 7.1, three variations from the current position are shown. Each produces a doubling of profit:

1   Increase sales by 25 per cent while holding fixed costs steady.
2   Hold sales steady while reducing direct costs by 12.5 per cent.
3   Increase average price by 5 per cent while holding volume and costs steady.

Table 7.1 Setting the price: three variations from the current position

	Current position	Increase sales	Lower costs	Increase price
Sales revenue £mn	10.0	12.5	10.0	10.5
Direct costs	6.0	7.5	5.5	6.0
Fixed costs	3.5	4.0	3.5	3.5
Net profit	0.5	1.0	1.0	1.0

Source: Example from Winkler 1983.

Of these three options, increasing the average price, perhaps by varying the product mix and introducing selective rises in some prices, is very much easier in practice than any of the others.

Since price is so important, it will again be the case that marketing alone is unlikely to have the final decision on pricing policy and exact prices set (except in some FMCG companies where marketing is the dominant function). What this chapter will examine is marketing's view of price, and why and how this marketing view should contribute to price setting. It will go on to explain different methods used in practice, and finally look at strategy and tactics in pricing.

MARKETING VIEW OF PRICE

Marketing people must of course understand the effect of price on profit; they must be thoroughly familiar with the cost–volume–profit relationship of their products – the way costs and profits vary with the volume produced and sold.

Beyond that, the marketing view of price should be different from that of the accountant or production manager. To marketing people, price is an element of the marketing mix, and they must take an external view: how is the price perceived by the three Cs with whom we are constantly concerned: customers, consumers and competitors?

It is vital that this distinction is maintained and understood. It is the customer's perception of our price that counts. The price is a piece of information, and it tells potential buyers something about the product even before they have bought it. Buyers do not always look just at the bare ticket price, but at the value for money that it represents in combination with this particular product and its supporting promotion and distribution.

When you next buy something, either for yourself or for the business (preferably both, if you can), think of the part price plays in your decision. The buying situations will vary, of course, and in some cases price may well be the determining factor in your choice. What sort of situation and product is that likely to be typical of? Almost certainly, one in which the available products are all very similar or identical in performance, are probably relatively low in price and unimportant in your life or business (paper clips, for example).

You will probably find that in most situations, price will be a consideration, but not the only one and not necessarily the most important. Even with mundane products such as toilet rolls, some people will always buy the cheapest, but many will pay a little extra for better quality as they perceive it. Most markets have a low-price, economy segment and a high-price, luxury segment, with most products somewhere in between. In some extreme cases, the high-price segment shows behaviour in which buyers choose *because* of the high price.

Use Worksheet 7.1 to record some of your buying decisions, commenting on the role of price in each.

There are a number of lessons to be drawn from a marketing view of price.

■ First, price is a signal of quality. It gives buyers expectations of the quality they will receive if they pay that amount. It is vital therefore that the price is consistent with the actual quality offered (part of the overall consistency of the marketing mix discussed in Chapter 5).

Marketing's role in pricing is therefore first of all to discover how buyers in the target segment judge value for money. We have seen

WORKSHEET 7.1 THE IMPORTANCE OF PRICE

■ Take some recent buying decisions you have made or contributed to (both domestic and business). Rank the importance of price in the decision (1 = most important), and comment on the other important factors.

Product	Rank of price	Comment (What had most impact, what was the relative role of price)

that this is not necessarily straightforward, since the buying and using situation may be more complex than at first appears. In a business situation a buyer may not choose the cheapest price, even when the products on offer are identical, preferring a supplier with a reputation for reliability and speed of delivery, for example. Again, the total cost of using a product may be different from the initial price; thus, Mercedes advertise to finance directors informing them that the total cost of buying Mercedes as company cars is actually lower than rivals, despite the higher initial price, because of the high trade-in value obtainable.

■ The second lesson is therefore that, in some buying situations, buyer perception of value may include not only the initial ticket price but the total cost of buying and using the product over its life time.

A further aspect of perception of value for money is that buyers must necessarily use competitors' prices as benchmarks when judging yours.

■ Your price and the perceived value for money it offers must always be seen relative to other prices prevailing in the market.

This may of course be an opportunity, if you can demonstrate that you do in fact offer better value for money in some way, remembering to see the customer's point of view and seeing the total cost of buying and using. For example, your price may be higher than competitors', but your superior applicator means less waste, and therefore lower cost per treatment in the end; or the way your service is delivered saves the buyer time (and therefore, by implication, money).

Finally, as price is an integral part of the overall part of the marketing mix, and therefore part of the product's positioning in its target segment, the pricing level once chosen cannot be altered quickly or often.

■ Pricing is a strategic decision; the price level of a brand cannot be changed significantly without reviewing and changing the whole strategy.

WORKSHEET 7.2 PRICES AGAINST COMPETITORS

■ Take your major products (in terms of sales and profits, from previous worksheets) and compare their prices with the range offered by competitors. Make allowances for differences in size, specification, etc. if possible.

■ Comment on:

1 The extent to which price differences reflect quality
2 What does explain price differences apart from obvious quality differences?

Product	Price	Range of competitor prices	Comment

In practice, few firms have the luxury of setting their prices completely freely. In most markets, price levels are established and difficult to change. To an extent, it is marketing's job to deliver some pricing freedom by building the brand's differentiation into a local monopoly. The more different and unique a brand, the more freedom it has in setting a price regardless of competition. This is one reason why finding and exploiting a point of difference *which is salient to consumers* is so crucial to marketing success.

Take your major products, and in Worksheet 7.2 compare their prices with your leading competitors. Do the differences represent real differences in quality, or something else?

PRICE SETTING METHODS

Cost-plus

The commonest method of setting prices is to calculate the total costs incurred in making and selling the product, adding some profit margin, and dividing by the total number of units you expect to sell. Since all costs have to be covered in the long run, this method ensures that such a consideration is built in to the pricing decision. It also has the virtue of simplicity.

The major disadvantage from a marketing point of view is that it takes no account of customers' perceptions or competitors' price levels – at least explicitly. In practice, a firm cannot ignore the marketplace, and would have to make adjustments if its pricing became out of line – by reducing the profit margin it is prepared to accept or by lowering costs in some way.

There is also a logical inconsistency in that the price is fixed by the number of units you expect to sell, but that number must be influenced by the price set.

A further problem was alluded to earlier, in Chapter 4, and that is the difficulty of allocating overhead costs. If overhead allocation is misleading it may lead to distortions in pricing and/or misleading profit figures for different products. Marketing people and accountants should work closely together in trying to understand the reality behind the standard cost figures, and their implications for pricing.

To sum up, cost-plus pricing is unsatisfactory from a marketing point of view, but a necessary input into the overall pricing decision.

Marginal pricing

The alternative to full-cost or cost-plus pricing is to calculate the marginal cost, that is, the cost of making one extra unit of the product; in practice this can be taken to be the variable cost. Managers can then work on the *contribution* (unit revenue minus variable cost) each product makes to overhead and profit.

Marginal pricing is popular as a concept with marketing people, since it seems to give them more freedom to allocate the contribution between marketing expenditure, overhead and profit; and because it seems to offer more freedom in pricing. Many accountants also approve, in principle at least, since it avoids the thorny problem of overhead allocation.

There are clear advantages to marginal pricing in certain defined situations, such as a potential order for an extra batch of product over and above normal production. In these circumstances, when overheads have in fact been covered, it makes sense to have the freedom to set a low price which will still make a positive contribution, and when only a price lower than would be set by cost-plus will gain the contract.

■ The danger for marketing managers is that in a normal customer situation they set a price which will be seen as a benchmark for future negotiation, and which will prevent the firm ever making an acceptable profit. From this viewpoint, marginal pricing should be seen as for exceptional rather than normal use.

Target pricing

This is an imprecise term that may mean one of a number of things, although always with the presumption that a target of some sort is involved in the pricing decision. Financial targets are common, such as margin (per cent of sales revenue), mark-up (per cent added to total cost, often used by professional service firms), or return on investment.

For marketing people, on the other hand, target pricing should refer to the target market and what it perceives as value for money. In marketing-oriented firms such as the Ford Motor Company, the price of a car is set early on in the development process in relation to consumer wants and competitors' prices; the car is then designed so that it can be manufactured profitably at that price.

Such market-oriented pricing is foreign to many managers from other departments, and particularly to engineers who regard 'designing down to a price' as somehow a betrayal. In fact, it is the discipline of the marketplace which is the challenge for all functions. If a target price set by the market is the focus for the challenges to be met, it is at least a clear and unambiguous one.

Competitive pricing

The need to be aware of competitors' prices has been mentioned several times. In most markets, the level of prices is framed by what competitors are offering, and only an exceptional product – such as a new invention protected by patents and in great demand from buyers – can ignore prevailing price levels.

Quite how closely competitors' prices have to be followed depends very much on the market situation. In some business-to-business relationships, the supplier and customer work together over long periods and are tied to each other in many ways.

Switching costs of moving to a new supplier may be high. In these circumstances, sales are probably not very sensitive to price; a competitor would have to come in with a very much lower price to tempt the customer. Conversely, if you are trying to break into new markets or gain new customers in this sort of market, small price differences will not be enough (in fact, you probably should not be competing on price anyway). This is sometimes a temptation to become complacent and to pad profit margins; a good customer will not allow that, and perhaps will ask for competing quotes every now and again to keep you on your toes.

In other markets, on the other hand, price competition is continuous and intense, and competitors' prices need to be monitored all the time.

The other major consideration is your standing in the market. Some firms are price leaders, and others price followers. Usually, but not always, the large company is the price leader and other firms have little choice but to follow. The advantage of being a leader is that you have the choice of timing price changes to suit yourself.

Finally, your company may have a fixed relationship to competitors' prices through its overall strategy. For example, you may offer a high-quality product which is always priced so much above named competitors; or, conversely, a low-priced (value-for-money) strategy with prices always so much below the market leader. Amstrad, for instance, prices its products to be noticeably below the other major manufacturers so that they always appear to be the best value for money on offer (this could also be interpreted as target pricing, but the exact label is unimportant).

Other approaches

Given the variety of market situations, there is not surprisingly a huge variety of detailed pricing methods which cannot be covered here. Two major considerations are noted.

Psychological pricing is often found in consumer markets; either the manufacturer or the retailer sets prices so that they are just below price points or shoulder prices, at which it is believed consumer resistance will set in. We are all familiar with prices such as £19.95. Setting prices in this way, at the lower level anyway, depends crucially on a sensitive knowledge of consumers and of competitors' prices. Given the effect on the bottom line of any price reduction, you must be certain that what you lose in margin you more than make up in sales volume.

At the other end of the spectrum, some prices are deliberately set very high, usually in luxury goods, to reinforce the positioning of status and prestige.

The other consideration, which applies in some markets, is that of geography. Where transport costs form an important part of total cost, the manufacturer may have to decide how to charge for them. In industries where this is true, there is often an established custom and practice. In larger markets, there is also the consideration of how to charge transport costs which are unequal between customers (average, actual, or zoned pricing are the options). Marketing's role should be to look at the customer's perception of value, and to look for ways of improving the total service.

Using Worksheet 7.3, examine the pricing methods used in your firm. What is marketing's role in the process? Comment on any improvements that could be made.

CHANNEL AND LINE PRICING

Although so far we have talked about the price of a product, in fact there are frequently at least two levels of price – one to the

WORKSHEET 7.3 PRICING METHODS

> ■ Taking the same products as in the previous worksheet, note what method has been used to set the price, and what marketing's role was in the process. In the comment column, draw any conclusions, particularly on improvements which could be made.
>
> | Product | Pricing method used | Marketing role | Comment |
> |---------|---------------------|----------------|---------|
> | | | | |

channel and one to the customer or consumer. The price charged to the distributor reflects the tasks carried out by that part of the chain, and also the relative power of the parties (see Chapter 9).

Again, in most industries there are accepted levels of margin for the wholesaler and retailers for each category of product. Very strong brands or leading companies may be able to offer margins lower than normal; conversely, a small manufacturer or someone trying to gain new distribution may have to offer higher margins.

The price charged to the middleman, and thus the margin allowed, is part of the continuing negotiation and bargaining process. As a principle, the manufacturer should give extra margin only when the distributor is giving some extra service, and there should be clear controls on the performance of the service. As we shall see in Chapter 9, this is not always easy.

Discounts, for example, should be structured so that it is clear what needs to be done to earn them. They should be motivating, not just there because that's the way it's always been done. An open price list, showing volume, payment and other discounts with their conditions, is preferable to secrecy, but does depend on the relative power of the supplier.

Line pricing is included here because there is frequently inter-action between pricing the product line and pricing for the channel. Where a manufacturer offers a number of products within a line, there is usually a range of prices and models from basic to premium. Normally, the margin for both manufacturer and channel is lowest for the basic model and highest for the top of the range. Obviously, the margin allowed for each product in the line should be such that it encourages the distributor to put most effort into those products you wish to sell most of.

STRATEGIES AND TACTICS IN PRICING

The pricing strategy of a company must, as has been pointed out, be part of its overall marketing strategy. The price cannot be seen in isolation; it is a part of the positioning and targeting strategy. Although a company may have a range of products and brands at different price levels (for example most car manufacturers), within each sector they will be in a pre-determined price band. This long-term strategy will have a constraining effect on pricing, as it is difficult to change price levels dramatically. It is noteworthy, for example, that the two major Japanese car manufacturers who have made a move into the luxury segment have both set up new and different brand names and distribution chains for these models; they clearly felt that consumers would not accept a very high price with a mass-market name, however good the product.

Opportunities for significant change at the strategic level, therefore, are few. One is introducing a genuinely new product which has no rivals for the time being. Then one has the choice of 'skimming' or 'penetration' pricing.

Skimming means skimming the cream from the market, and suggests setting a high price and earning a high margin while the going is good. New drugs under patent protection often take this route, as did the Polaroid instant camera.

Penetration, on the other hand, suggests that you recognise that competition will follow swiftly and that the market will develop rapidly; you set a relatively low price to gain sales fast and establish a leading position in the marketplace. Which strategy is chosen clearly depends on your interpretation of how the market is going to develop, and how competitors will react; often this demands great flair and judgement, as no market research will tell you. If you are entering new markets (new countries, for example) you may have the experience from elsewhere to go on, and you may be able to use the experience from similar products; but it is still a delicate decision.

Tactics in pricing are concerned with timing: when to make price changes up or down to gain some tactical advantage or defend yourself against competitors.

Price rises should ideally be made at the same time as quality improvement so that the package can be presented as a whole (in 1993 for example the *Independent* newspaper raised its cover price at the same time that it introduced colour and a second section). A rise can be delayed behind competitors if it is felt that the market is price-sensitive; or alternatively made ahead of competitors to gain additional margin if price sensitivity is not thought to be high. Customers should be warned of price rises so that they can build them into their cost calculations.

Price cuts can again be used as a tactical weapon, either temporarily or, if costs have fallen permanently, for the longer term. The marketing task is, as always, to determine how the price cut will be perceived. How will consumers and competitors react? Depending on the market, a small cut may have little or no effect; but a large one may produce a heavy competitive reaction. Will buyers stock up during a temporary price cut and then buy less next period? Will they interpret the cut as only the first step, and wait for further cuts?

The worst scenario is that a cut will start a price war which nobody will win. Such a move should be made only by a very strong competitor certain that all the others will lose more than the initiator; even then, it is a risky tactic. Compaq adopted a price-cutting strategy successfully in the personal computer market, but in that very dynamic situation the plan could easily have failed. From time to time the major supermarket multiples engage in price wars, though it has to be said that so far they have been relatively gentle affairs: it remains to be seen what will happen when severe price competition from discounters and warehouse clubs offers a real threat.

In general, the firm should have a pricing policy which tells it how to react in given circumstances – when the price leader lowers its price, for instance. Such a policy should be based on detailed calculations of the effects – on sales and profits – of different actions. A well-prepared company will react more quickly and with better information than one relying on instinct or luck.

Examine some recent price changes made by your company, using Worksheet 7.4, and see how well prepared they were. Did they have the effects intended, or was there some unplanned loss of sales or profit? How could you do better (assuming you are not already perfect)?

WORKSHEET 7.4 POLICY ON PRICING CHANGES

■   Find some recent examples of price changes made by your company. Establish whether the change was initiated by a competitor or by your company; and if by your company, by which department (marketing, finance, production, other). Rate how well prepared you think the price change was (amount of analysis done, conformed to well-established policy etc.). Comment on the results: were they as expected, or was there some loss (or gain) in sales compared with expectations?

Product	Price change	Initiated by:	How well prepared	Comment

8 Communicating with markets

What do we want to communicate, to whom and how?

All organisations need to communicate with the outside world all the time. A typical firm will have a large number of audiences with which it wishes to communicate, including shareholders and potential investors, the City, government, opinion leaders, suppliers and its own employees. Marketing is not directly concerned with these audiences, so they will not be dealt with here, though that is not to deny their importance.

On the other hand, marketing is concerned with all communications between the company and its markets. That includes not only the obvious means such as advertising, sales promotion and personal selling – which are dealt with in this chapter – but every communication that takes place and which gives information to buyers and potential buyers. The way the telephone is answered, the way people take messages and pass them on (or not), how accountants deal with queries, perhaps even the state of the company's lorries and the road manners of its drivers – all are forms of communication.

This can be a frightening realisation, since it is extremely difficult if not impossible to control all these; yet they may be affecting buying decisions over time. It is this sort of view which leads companies such as British Airways to put all its employees through customer care programmes; total quality programmes can have the same effect, of making everyone realise that they are part of the way the firm communicates, and that everyone has customers.

This chapter will, more prosaically, examine the main methods marketing uses to communicate with markets: advertising, promotion and personal selling, with a particular note on the rising medium of direct marketing.

THE COMMUNICATIONS MIX

As we talk about the various tools making up the marketing mix, so we use the term communications mix to refer to all the various media we choose to communicate with our markets and the way we balance them.

The media available are, in broad terms:

- advertising
- promotion
- personal selling
- public relations
- other publicity

To take the last first, other publicity covers the huge range of ways business people have thought of to publicise their products. Given the ingenuity and dedication expended, this covers almost everything, from human beings themselves (sports players), through virtually every object whether moving or fixed (deckchairs, matchboxes, buildings, buses ...) to the air itself (sky-writing). The range cannot even be listed here as it is so vast. The way all should be evaluated is exactly the same as we shall apply in this chapter to the more conventional media: what is it trying to achieve, how well does it do it, how does it fit in with the rest of the mix?

Public relations, too, is a large topic which cannot be covered in detail here. Its range extends to communications outside the marketing field, such as investor relations, and although it is often used as an adjunct to a marketing campaign, it really deserves study in its own right. In marketing, it is often used to gain press coverage in support of a campaign, particularly when the subject is sensitive and advertising is controlled or limited (for example, where health claims are concerned).

In approaching the communications mix, the company should start by analysing:

- What audiences we are trying to reach
- What messages we wish to send to each
- What media are available which could reach the audience
- The effectiveness and efficiency of each

It can then go on to:

■ Choose a medium for each message for each audience (there may be more than one message and more than one medium for each audience)
■ Check the consistency and coherence of the mix (are they all saying the same thing, not contradicting each other?)
■ Check the fit with the rest of the marketing mix (again using the tests of consistency and coherence)

Try part of this yourself for your own company, using Worksheet 8.1. Are all the audiences covered, and all the messages getting through? Do you know how effective and efficient the communications mix is? Do you think it could be improved?

WORKSHEET 8.1 AUDIENCES AND MEDIA

■ List the audiences with which your firm communicates (or ought to). Be as specific as possible (e.g. engineering directors of machine-tool manufacturers with a turnover of less than £100 million; or females aged between 25 and 45 who earn more than £30,000 a year and may need pensions advice). Summarise the message(s) you think are being communicated to each, and the media used. There may be more than one message per audience, and more than one medium per message. Try to think of alternative media which could also be used.

Audience	Messages to be communicated	Media used	Alternative media

ADVERTISING: WHAT IT CAN AND CAN'T DO

Advertising is the most visible part of marketing activity. We are all bombarded with advertising messages all the time; we consume vast quantities of it, some more willingly than others. We all have our favourite advertisements – and probably our least favourite ones too. Advertising is an inescapable part of our lives, and an important part of our culture. To some extent, we all feel that we know a lot about it.

In reality, we actually know surprisingly little about how advertising works. For most firms, it is a comparatively small part of their marketing expenditure. Even those – mainly consumer goods manufacturers – who spend considerable sums on it do not know as much as they would like to about its effects.

If you look around at a sample of the advertising to which you are exposed, it is clear that many things are being attempted. An advertising campaign may be trying to:

- introduce a new brand
- inform users of a product modification
- remind users of the benefits
- get non-users to try the product
- inform about a special offer
- persuade users to use more
- suggest new uses
- increase the perceived importance of certain attributes of the brand
- stress advantages against competitors
- present technical information
- present general company characteristics (size, reputation, research record etc.)
- and many others

What we need to understand is how the advertising relates to the marketing strategy and objectives of the firm. Advertising does not have a separate life and justification of its own: it must be seen in the context of the rest of the marketing mix as contributing to sales and profits.

Unfortunately, this is where the difficulties start. To say that advertising must justify itself by its contribution to profits is true, but not very helpful, since as with any element of the mix it is extremely difficult to measure exactly what advertising's part is. As was argued in Chapter 4, this is an area in which controlled experimentation can help to provide answers, and large sophisticated firms have been doing this over many years. In other cases, as with press advertisements carrying coupon replies, measurement is straightforward. For most firms, however, little real information is available and some interim information must be used.

Most advertising objectives, although related to marketing objectives such as market share, are translated into communications objectives: imparting some piece of information, or improving buyers' ratings of brand attributes. Such communication can be measured using market research. The difficulty is making the connection between improved attitudes to the brand and improved sales. There is some evidence that liking for a brand is related to buying it, but generalised evidence as to how advertising makes people buy is limited.

One argument is that all advertising can do is:

■ raise *awareness*
■ encourage *trial*
■ encourage *repeat buying*

This ATR model is based on extensive research into buying patterns (mentioned in Chapter 3 above). It is thought of as a 'weak' theory of advertising; but most people who have worked in the field do not believe that advertising is capable of enormous impact. What we do know is that advertising, as opposed to promotions (see below), can have a measurable effect on sales over two to three years; this does not make the task of evaluating its impact any easier, but it does back up the view of advertising as an investment in the brand.

The number of campaigns which have been truly great, and have changed markets dramatically, is very small indeed (the number of truly bad campaigns, which have ruined a brand, are fortunately even fewer in number, though they have occurred). Although it is tempting to be very rational and to specify exactly what the advertising campaign should be communicating and why, this is not always possible. One of the longest-running and (presumably) most effective campaigns on British television has chimpanzees dressed up as humans, dubbed to act out amusing scenes. Quite how that relates to communicating the benefits of the particular brand of tea it is advertising is unclear (to this observer at least). It is reinforcing an image of humour and friendliness, and perhaps of a particular sort of Britishness which is associated with tea drinking, and to that extent can be said to be strengthening brand associations and values.

Perhaps we should leave the creation of advertising to the people who may know some things unconsciously that we cannot know intellectually. That is not to say that managers should abandon responsibility; they must work out the role of advertising within the overall marketing mix and assign specific objectives to it; as will be argued in the next section, they must make judgements and take decisions.

Most of this discussion has implicitly at least been about consumer advertising, since that is where most expenditure is. Advertising has a place in business marketing too, however. At the very least, it can introduce the company and its products to its target audiences, so that when the sales person calls it is not completely cold. Advertising may also be used to reach people in the decision-making unit other than those called on by the sales team, and to transmit different messages: to tell the finance director about economic issues while the sales people concentrate on technical matters, for example.

Take one or more of your company's advertisements or campaigns, and specify exactly what task you think it was carrying out; record this in Worksheet 8.2. Check your view with that of the person responsible for the advertising, and if possible with a member of the target audience. Are there any discrepancies?

ADVERTISING DECISIONS

There are four main decisions to be taken about advertising, and they are inter-related:

- size of the budget
- media to be used
- content of the message
- creative treatment

WORKSHEET 8.2 ADVERTISING TASKS

> ■ Pick one or more recent advertisements or advertising campaigns that your firm has run. Write down what exactly you think it was trying to achieve; be as specific as possible. Then find out which manager was responsible for commissioning the advertising, and ask him or her what the objectives were. Finally, if possible ask one or more customers what they thought. Compare the results, and draw conclusions.

Name of ad/campaign	Tasks/objectives you think advertising had	What manager responsible says	What customer thinks

They are inter-related because one may enter the circle at any point. A particular message, which is determined by the overall marketing strategy, may need a particular medium; a highly technical message with many details needs print, for example, while a novel product demonstration may demand television. Alternatively, only a certain amount of money may be available, thereby cutting out expensive media such as TV.

Size of the budget

The common methods used to fix the budget are:

■ percentage of sales
■ what we can afford
■ competitive parity
■ objective and task
■ mathematical model

The last two are the most rational, but only a large and sophisticated company which spends heavily on advertising is likely to have devoted the time and resources to developing such a model. The objective and task approach is appealing excet that, as we have seen, it is not always clear how we can set and measure such objectives.

Most companies probably use one of the first two, even if they are not logical methods. The percentage-of-sales method suffers from the same problem as the cost-plus approach to pricing: expected sales are used to decide on the advertising spend, but the advertising spend ought to affect the amount of sales we achieve. Despite this, the method is popular, as it is simple. Where advertising forms only a small part of the total budget and has limited aims, it is probably good enough.

The other methods are self-explanatory. In many cases, a mixture of more than one method may be used.

Media selection

Choice of media is in some ways more straightforward. What we need to know is what audience we are trying to reach, and what audience each competing media vehicle delivers at what cost. We can then choose the most efficient in terms of cost per thousand target audience.

Most media houses publish figures on their audience, ranging from the very full details produced for the TV industry and national press to home-produced circulation and readership figures published by some small publications. Where data are produced by the publication itself, some caution should be used in evaluating them; audited circulation figures may be better than doubtful readership claims.

More qualitative issues may arise, such as the suitability of a particular media vehicle for a particular advertisement. Some judgement may be necessary, especially where a medium justifies a higher price by claiming greater authority and therefore effectiveness.

Message content

The general content – what overall message you want this particular audience to receive – is the responsibility of marketing management. It must fit into the rest of the mix, and it should be clear what exactly advertising's unique role in the task is.

Message treatment

We have argued that this is the job of creative people, probably in the specialist advertising agency which your company employs for the purpose. Nevertheless, your management must judge the proposals put to them.

Some guideline questions which they may use are:

- Does it meet the brief?
- Is it consistent with the company and brand positioning?
- Does it communicate the message?
- Does it address the target audience's concerns? (Remember the product-in-use, and the way your brand fits in with the consumer's life.)
- Does it talk the language and use the tone of voice appropriate to the audience?
- Will it stand out?
- Will it work?

The last is, of course, the most difficult question of all, and in the end is a matter of confidence in the creative team and in your own judgement.

Use Worksheet 8.3 to evaluate one of your own company's advertising campaigns.

PROMOTION

In marketing the term promotion is used in a specific sense, distinguished from advertising. If advertising is persuasive communication in paid-for media (i.e. what we usually mean when we talk of advertisements), then promotion covers all other attempts to promote the product or the firm apart from advertising and personal selling.

The main categories are:

- sponsorship
- packaging
- displays
- point-of-purchase promotion
- demonstrations
- free samples

WORKSHEET 8.3 EVALUATING AN ADVERTISING CAMPAIGN

■ Take a recent campaign your firm has run (perhaps the one you used in the Worksheet 8.2), and evaluate it using the criteria below. You may like to compare your views with those of the manager responsible.

Advertisement/campaign ....

1 Does it meet the brief?

2 Is it consistent with the company and brand positioning?

3 Does it communicate the message?

4 Does it address the target audience's concerns? (remember the product-in-use, and the way your brand fits in with the consumer's life)

5 Does it talk the language and use the tone of voice appropriate to the audience?

6 Will it stand out?

7 Will it work?

■ premium offers (gifts, extra product etc.)
■ competitions
■ exhibitions and trade fairs
■ other material (brochures, leaflets, films etc.)

These different methods clearly have different applications. Some – point-of-purchase, free samples, competitions – are normally associated with consumer goods, while others – exhibitions and trade fairs, brochures – are more likely to be found in industrial markets.

There is now a good deal of evidence that well planned promotions can have dramatic short-term effects on sales of consumer brands: increases of five or ten times normal volumes are possible.

On the other hand, such effects are short-term. The periods following a successful promotion may see a corresponding drop in sales, as the buyers who would have bought anyway and who stocked up during the promotion miss a purchase; and the general level of sales soon returns to normal.

What the promotion hopes to do is to entice some buyers who would not normally buy the brand, and keep some of them when the promotion is over. As we know that most buyers in fact buy a repertoire of brands in any one product field, what the promotion can do is to convert some less-frequent buyers of your brand into more-frequent buyers – assuming that your brand is of a quality that their experience of it in use is convincing.

There is a danger that promotion can be over used. Pressure from retailers, allied to the fast-rising cost of some advertising media, has led to a shift of marketing funds 'below the line', that is from advertising to promotion. Too much reliance on promotion can carry the unconscious message that the brand alone is not good enough to persuade people to buy: they must be offered some extra incentive. While this is clearly not intended, it may be implicit.

Promotion therefore should be used sparingly, to add excitement and visibility to a brand. Wherever possible, the promotion should be relevant to the brand rather than completely unconnected; and it should reinforce not go against the brand's values.

As with all the other elements, promotion must be consistent and coherent with the rest of the mix. Judging by successful promotions (and advertising), we ought to look for another three Cs to match our customers, consumers and competitors:

- consistency
- coherence
- creativity

As with advertising, evaluate one or more uses of promotion by your company, using Worksheet 8.4.

DIRECT MARKETING

The fastest-growing area of marketing communication in recent

WORKSHEET 8.4 EVALUATING A PROMOTION

■ Choose some promotion (anything other than advertising and personal selling) used by your company recently, and evaluate it. Again, compare your conclusions with the manager responsible if possible.

Promotion (name) ....

Type (premium offer, competition etc.) ....

1 Target audience
2 Relevance of promotion to target audience
3 Relevance to the brand
4 Rating for:
      Consistency (with strategy)
      Coherence (with rest of mix)
      Creativity
5 Effect on sales (if possible)
6 Cost-effectiveness

Conclusion

---

years has been direct marketing. Growing out of direct mail and mail order, direct marketing is now a large and sophisticated business in its own right, as well as a set of techniques which an increasing number of firms in different markets are adopting.

The key words in the jargon surrounding the subject are:

■ direct, and
■ database

It is the availability of cheap computing power that has allowed direct marketing to improve its efficiency. Essentially, the marketing company builds up a database on its customers and potential customers. This can record not only basics such as name and address, but previous responses to campaigns, and details of purchases. Data from various sources, such as mailing lists bought from the many suppliers, can be used as a basis, but mainly the company builds up data from its own mailings. Anyone who has ever received material from Readers' Digest or the Consumers' Association will know how sophisticated some of the material is.

In industrial markets, too, database marketing can improve targeting and efficiency. As a small example, the office stationery company from which I buy my supplies sends me personalised mailings saying, for instance, 'On 24 July 1992 you bought bubblejet ink cartridges at £16.79 each ... Buy now at only £13.99.' This sums up the advantages of the approach: it can use a detailed record of each customer's purchases to stimulate further buying, target particular campaigns very precisely, and measure their effects so as to guide future actions.

PERSONAL SELLING

The sales force remains for many companies the main method of communicating with markets. Sales people are expensive, but there are many tasks which only they can perform. Especially in markets in which the products are highly technical, and the relationship between supplier and customer is close and long-standing, there is no substitute for personal contact.

There have been changes to the old, traditional sales force in some markets, however. The large sales force, several hundred strong, calling on all grocery stores on behalf of consumer goods manufacturers, hardly exists any more. Instead, there is a much smaller number of higher-quality, better-trained people negotiating with the head offices of retail multiples. In this, the new sales force is much closer to that found in the industrial field: the role is more to do with managing the relationship over time to the mutual benefit of the partners than hard selling.

The other factors which have changed the role of some sales forces are technological. The telephone is now used for a great deal of routine re-ordering and initial customer contact in both consumer and business-to-business markets, being much cheaper than sales people on the road and perfectly effective for some tasks.

The newer development is electric data interchange, by which the computer systems of supplier and customer are linked directly. Much of the routine detail of ordering and processing is then carried out automatically.

None of this should be thought to detract from the enormously important role that personal selling has in many areas of industry. Cost pressures may, however, mean that existing ways of doing things are challenged, and decisions on, for example, the size and allocation of the sales force are not immune.

The size of a sales force is traditionally decided by the number of existing and potential customers divided by the number of calls a sales person can be expected to make in this market. The logic of this is unassailable, but it is worth challenging some of the assumptions. Do all the tasks need to be carried out in person (rather than by telephone or direct marketing)? Is the traditional number of calls the most efficient, or would varying it for different classes of customer improve the cost per sale ratio?

In terms of allocation of effort, too, questions should be asked. Are we calling on the right companies? On the right people within those companies? Does our allocation of effort as between existing and new customers reflect our overall marketing strategy?

Organisation structure must also reflect changes in markets. The old regional structure may no longer be appropriate; should we instead have national account managers looking after the major customers? Is a product-based or market-based organisation more suited to current needs?

The key here, as throughout the marketing process, is to go back constantly to the market. The personal selling effort must be geared to maintaining the vital relationship between our customers and the firm. The sales people are the eyes and ears of the company, an essential part of a two-way communication system. Being so expensive, they must be carefully targeted, and should concentrate their efforts on tasks that only they can perform.

As with all the other elements, the selling effort must be co-ordinated with the rest of the marketing mix. Unfortunately, in many firms this is not done, partly because of historical rivalry between sales and other functions, particularly marketing! Such rivalries must not be allowed to get in the way of the teamwork which is essential to delivering quality service to customers.

Examine your own personal selling effort, and how it fits in with the rest of the communications mix and the overall marketing mix.

WORKSHEET 8.5 EVALUATING THE SALES FORCE

■ Describe the current size and structure of your sales force. Try to find out what its objectives and tasks are (*specifically*). Evaluate how well these objectives are being met, and whether they could be met better in any other way.

Size of sales force ....

Structure (regional, product-based, customer-based etc.)

Specific objectives and tasks	*How well met/carried out*	*Alternative ways of carrying out*

How well is selling effort integrated with rest of marketing mix?

Conclusions

Although this is probably a major task, you may wish to evaluate its current role using Worksheet 8.5.

9 Distributing the products

Getting our products to the right place at the right time

Every manufacturer needs to distribute the product somehow. Services companies also need some form of distribution, either direct or through intermediaries, for example insurance products sold through brokers and agents. In this chapter we will talk entirely about physical products, but the same principles apply to services.

Some manufacturers distribute directly, others, perhaps most, through intermediaries. This chapter discusses the types and functions of channels or intermediaries, and the way suppliers should manage the relationship.

WHAT INTERMEDIARIES DO

The various types of channel or intermediary that exist (including wholesalers, retailers, agents, brokers, jobbers, and industrial distributors of various sorts) perform some set of a number of functions:

- *Physical distribution*
- *Matching* (making available the assortment of goods from different suppliers wanted by the channel's customers)
- *Time and place utility* (ensuring the assortment is available where and when wanted)
- *Finance* (during the time the product spends in the channel; though note that this is emphatically not true of retailers of fast-moving consumer goods, who normally sell the goods before they pay for them)
- *Transfer of title* (ensuring that legal ownership passes)
- *Risk-bearing* (sharing some of the risk inherent in business)
- *Research and prospecting* (for customers and what they want)

- *Promotion and selling*
- *Service*
- *Support services* (insurance, documentation etc.)

Exactly which set of functions a particular intermediary performs will depend to a large extent on the history of the industry. Normally each industry has an established structure, with more or less specialised firms carrying out sets of channel tasks.

The length of the distribution chain can vary from zero level (direct distribution) through one, two or three levels (e.g. manufacturer–wholesaler–jobber–retailer). What are called vertical marketing systems are integrated multi-level systems such as owned or contractually tied outlets (e.g. pubs in Britain), or franchises in the specific sense of, say, car main dealers or Coca-Cola bottlers.

However simple or complicated the system, all its members have two, sometimes conflicting, characteristics: they are all:

- Independent businesses trying to make a profit
- Members of the same system who will all do better if the system as a whole does better

All the members are to an extent fighting for their share of the total value added or profit generated by the chain as a whole. Frequently this leads to adversarial relationships marked by a concentration on prices and margins. The more constructive approach which is seen in some areas is for the members at different levels to see each other as partners working for their mutual benefit. If they can jointly improve the efficiency and effectiveness of the system, they both stand to gain.

Use Worksheet 9.1 to describe the distribution structure of your industry, and the tasks carried out by each level. Is the general atmosphere one of co-operation or conflict?

CHOOSING AND MANAGING INTERMEDIARIES

In many cases, there is in practice little choice of channel, as the industry structure is well established. Occasionally a firm will break out of the existing pattern, as Avon did by distributing cosmetics direct to consumers, and Family Circle did by selling its magazine in supermarkets.

WORKSHEET 9.1 DISTRIBUTION STRUCTURE

■ Describe the distribution structure of your industry, ticking which tasks are carried out by which level and type of intermediary. Then give a view of the general atmosphere prevailing between parties on the scale from co-operation to conflict; try to explain why this particular state of affairs exists.

Levels of intermediary (fill in)

——— ——— ——— ———

Tasks

1 Physical distribution
2 Matching
3 Time and place utility
4 Finance
5 Transfer of title
6 Risk-bearing
7 Research and prospecting
8 Promotion and selling
9 Service
10 Support services

General atmosphere

Conflict ——————————————————— *Co-operation*

■ Why is this so?

These examples show that it is sometimes worth looking hard at the present structure and testing to see if any advantage can be gained by challenging it. In most cases, though, the choice is restricted to the channels which are there.

Let us assume that you are making a choice of distributor for the first time, or reviewing your existing arrangements. How do you go about choosing or evaluating?

■ First, the distributor must above all deliver access to your target market. Your marketing strategy will have decided whether you are going for a mass market, or for limited distribution in exclusive outlets to reach the luxury segment, for example. In industrial markets, the distributor must cover the industries, geographical areas and types of firm you have selected.

■ Second, the chosen partner must be able to offer the level of service you believe the product needs to support it. In selling personal computers, some suppliers use distributors big enough to provide back-up advice and service to buyers; others sell through minimum service channels such as mail order.

■ Third, how much profit will you make out of the relationship? In some cases you may trade off margin for volume, but in every case you need to make a satisfactory level of profit – and so does the distributor.

Beyond these criteria, normal business judgement needs to be exercised as to the financial soundness, reputation, quality of management and so on of your proposed partner.

Remember that choosing a distribution channel is a *strategic* decision: it is part of the implementation of the overall strategy, and it is a long-term commitment which cannot be changed easily. It deserves careful thought and investigation.

Managing the relationship

The ideal, as has been suggested, is that both partners gain the maximum from the relationship. Major car manufacturers, and others such as JCB in earth-moving equipment, have invested heavily in their dealers. They may provide management training, business services such as software systems, even design. The result is that the dealer is a better-run, more efficient business, and it sells more of the product, so both parties win.

In any successful partnership, it helps to define what each party's responsibilities are. In the case of distribution, the supplier can be expected to provide given levels of customer service: frequency and timing of delivery, response time, correctness of delivery, accuracy of invoicing, and so on.

■ It is essential to define customer service from the customer's point of view. In one major manufacturer, the account managers were unable to show the company's customer service figures to their customers, because they were defined entirely from the manufacturer's point of view, and therefore quite unrepresentative of the customer's actual experience. For example, if the customer asked for certain products which the company knew it could not supply for the moment, that was not counted as an error by the manufacturer, although to the customer it was a clear shortfall in service.

The distributor, on the other hand, should also have standards of service, defined in terms of stocking, display, promotion, after-sales service and so on as appropriate. Where discounts are negotiated for the performance of certain services, these should be monitored before the discounts are granted.

Using Worksheet 9.2, list the customer service elements and levels your firm expects from its distributors, and the elements and levels it demands in return. Is the relationship an equal one, or is one party getting more than the other? If there is little or no definition of service levels, would it make the relationship more effective if there were?

The major problem likely to be encountered with distributors, apart from the issue of retailer power discussed below, is that of motivation and commitment. Most distributors will stock the products of several rival suppliers in any one field. What each supplier wants is for the distributor to be very committed to *their* relationship and products, and to give them preferential support. A distributor may be willing to do this, but usually only if the margin is better than that of rivals. This is equivalent to getting into a price war, as giving a better margin is in effect a price cut, and is easily copied (it also has an immediate and lasting effect on the bottom line).

■ A more positive approach is to try to enhance the quality of the relationship by applying marketing thinking to the distributor as a customer. What do they really want from you? Do you actually know? Have you ever asked them how you could improve the service you give, and how you could work together to improve the business?

WORKSHEET 9.2 SERVICE LEVELS

■ Define the elements of service and the level of each expected of your firm by its distributors, and similarly for what you expect from your distributors (e.g. correctness of deliveries is an element, and 90 per cent correct against order is the service level set; what you expect from a distributor may be holding stock, with a service level of no more than ten stock-outs per year).

Your firm to distributors

Elements of
service   Service level

Distributors to your firm

Elements of
service   Service level

Conclusions

Some demands may of course be impossible to meet; but marketing, as we saw in the first chapter, is not about merely giving people what they want, but matching our offering as closely as possible to customer needs while meeting our own objectives for profit. Actually listening to distributors, and treating them as customers rather than as an inert channel through which your goods pass to your final buyers, is an excellent start to a new way of managing the relationship.

In many consumer markets, this has been forced on reluctant manufacturers by the growing power of retailers; this is discussed in the next section.

COPING WITH RETAILER POWER

In many consumer markets, the last twenty years have seen a revolution in retailing. The spectacular growth of retail multiples in groceries, DIY, electrical products, clothes, drugs and many others has produced a quite new situation in marketing terms.

In the 1960s the mass consumer manufacturers were the power in the market. They invested large sums in product development and advertising, they managed major brands which consumers wanted to buy. They more or less told retailers what to do, treating them as a channel not as partners.

The power of the multiples now is such that in many fields a small number of firms control the majority of the market. In groceries, where the phenomenon is best seen, the top three – Sainsbury's, Tesco and Safeway – control half the packaged grocery market (and much more in some areas and product fields). Their management is now sophisticated and well trained, and their operations run with very high levels of efficiency.

Buying decisions are now highly centralised, and made at head office by high-quality teams with access to tremendous amounts of information through their EPOS (electronic point-of-sale) systems.

Retailers' brands are now more than just cheap imitations of manufacturers' brands; many are quality brands in their own right, highly regarded by consumers. This, and the way that retail power has diverted marketing spending from above-the-line support for brands (that is, theme advertising) to promotional spending, much of it controlled by the retailer, is a real threat to manufacturers' traditional brands.

In these circumstances, the balance of power has changed completely, with retailers now in the driving seat, making increasing demands on suppliers for better margins, increased promotional support and better customer service. For a time many manufacturers found it hard to adjust to this new situation, and open warfare seemed imminent. The majority of manufacturers, led by those who saw the light first, have adapted their strategies and often their structure. They are trying to develop real partnerships, and treating the relationship with customers as a potentially positive one. In other words, they are applying marketing thinking to customers as well as to consumers, and are adopting the ways of thinking and acting that many industrial marketers have been using for years.

In a fuller discussion of this topic (Randall 1990; 1993) I recommended that manufacturers should go through the following checklist of steps.

- *Understand your consumers*: who they are, what they want, what part your brands play in their lives, how they use them, what benefits are important to them, what is missing.
- *Look into the future*: identify the factors that are producing change in your consumers, and predict how this will affect your markets.
- *Understand your competitors*: analyse the structure of your markets, and identify the forces which are driving change.
- *Understand your customers*: who they are, what their strategies are, where your brands fit within those strategies, what their problems and opportunities are and how you can help them.
- *Build an information system*: identify all the information you need to guide your strategy, help your decision making and implement and control your plans; make sure that the right information is available to the people who need it when they need it. This will include information on customers and competitors, and on international and external trends, as well as straight market data. Because of the demands of the new customer relationships, it will also include internal cost data from manufacturing and distribution, perhaps in new forms; it should include customer profitability data.
- *Analyse your brand portfolio*: be realistic about the future of each of your brands, given the data on consumers, customers and competitors you have gathered. Which will definitely survive as major brands, which will need a lot of remedial help, which are in danger? Check that you will generate the cash necessary to support the brands in the way they will need.
- *Develop a brand strategy*: decide on the actions needed over the next few years to achieve your objectives; decide on whether or not to make retailers' brands.
- *Develop a customer strategy*: take a stance on whether you will be a strong independent, a partner, or a responsive supplier. Target the major customer groups and accounts, deciding on a strategy for each.
- *Fix clear objectives and budgets for brands and customers*: decide what is needed to achieve your objectives, set budgets and allocate responsibility for decisions on spending. Make people accountable.

■ *Think customers*: make sure that customer thinking penetrates deeply into the company, into all the departments whose activities do affect the relationship even if they are not yet aware of it.

■ *Rethink your organisation structure*: make sure that your structure helps you to deliver the information and actions needed to implement your strategies. List the tasks that relate to customers and allocate them to those best able to carry them out (not necessarily those whose job it has traditionally been).

■ *Build business teams*: make sure that everyone who contributes to the total delivery of a brand to customers and consumers is involved. Make sure that information flows within the team so that action can be coordinated.

■ *Improve the quality of the people dealing with customer service*: managers dealing with major retailers must be of a calibre and status equal to those in brand development.

■ *Implement a training programme*: ensure that NAMs (national account managers) and others dealing with customers are fully trained in DPP (direct product profitability) and space management models, and in negotiation and presentation skills. Use training to implant customer thinking and build teams.

■ *Review recruitment and selection policies*: decide what sort of people are going to be needed not just today but in the future in your new organisation. Plan to have them available and prepared. Ensure that all marketing managers have significant experience dealing with customers.

As so often in business, changes which seem threatening also offer opportunities to alert companies. The issue of retailer power is an enormous threat, but it does give the manufacturer who responds quickly the chance to gain a real competitive advantage.

ELECTRONICS AND SOME ACRONYMS

Some aspects of the way electronics have contributed to the retailing revolution have been mentioned. They will be drawn together here and some jargon explained, as the impact on all levels of distribution is so important. All suppliers need to understand what is happening so that they can adapt to it in managing their relationships with distributors successfully.

EPOS refers to any electronic point-of-sale system, but it is seen at its most effective in the scanning systems noticeable in more and more stores (and other levels of the distribution chain). Scanning captures huge amounts of detailed data, so that the user can potentially know exactly how many of each SKU (stocking unit, or one size of one variety of one brand for example) at any time. Sales by item are recorded and can be analysed by time of day, day of week, store, region, promotional activity, price ... and so on almost *ad infinitum*. The potential of this data source is huge, and the only problem is likely to be the software and people to interpret it.

For manufacturers, there is the issue that retailers now have much more information about sales of their products than they do (even if only within one chain). Some retailers are prepared to sell the data (or some of it) to a common processor such as a market research company, but others are not.

EDI has also been mentioned. It allows the computers of suppliers and distributors to communicate directly, and clearly has great potential in saving time and cutting out error. It is spreading fast in Britain, and is moving from exchange of information to direct ordering. It is also, interestingly, driving the development of real partnerships between suppliers and retailers advocated earlier in this chapter.

DPP (direct product profitability) is the application of management accounting ideas to the movement of product through the factory and distribution chain. As products are of different sizes and shapes, they take up different amounts of cubic space. They also vary in the ease with which they can be shifted, stored and displayed. DPP allows the retailer to calculate the real profit on each product allowing for all these differences. It is not yet used in negotiations between manufacturers and retailers, but may be in future.

In the USA, electronic systems have gone further than in the UK. There are systems which allow the price displayed on electronic tags on shelves to be changed in all a company's stores all over the USA simultaneously. There are also many other developments in in-store automation and integrated systems.

The lesson from a marketing point of view is that anything which makes the distribution chain more efficient must be good for all parties. What manufacturers need to do is to look for the opportunities offered by new developments to give a better service to their customers, by adapting their systems and anticipating the effect of their actions on their customers.

10 Putting it all together
Strategy and planning

In the previous chapters we have necessarily had to discuss the various parts of marketing separately. In reality, of course, they should all work together to achieve the firm's goals. To make sure that this actually happens is the purpose of strategy and planning; in this final chapter we will see how all the previous analyses fit together into a common framework, within the company's overall planning system.

STRATEGY

The word strategy has become somewhat over-used in the last few years. In particular, it has often been the rather pompous way of justifying in hindsight what a manager happens to have done successfully.

For a strategy to have any meaning, two things are necessary:

- A set of goals or objectives
- A clear statement of how the company is going to compete in its chosen markets in the medium term (i.e. longer than one year)

Thus a marketing strategy must have specified objectives, and that in turn implies that the objectives must relate to the firm's overall goals. A marketing strategy cannot exist in isolation, but only as part of a business strategy.

If the business does not have a strategy, or at least not one which is articulated and preferably written down, does that mean that marketing cannot think and act strategically? In theory, it does; but life has to go on, and it may be that in developing a marketing strategy the manager has to make assumptions which can be tested with senior managers (and may indeed prompt them to think further about the business strategy).

The other interaction between marketing and business strategy is that, although the overall business strategy must guide what marketing does, parts of it must in its turn be guided by marketing analysis and thought. In particular, the choice of product-market scope – what products we aim at which markets – is fundamental to business strategy but must be based on marketing analysis of what forces are driving the different markets under consideration.

The strategy process is *iterative*, that is, it goes through several cycles, with a subsidiary part of the process feeding back to an earlier level. Especially when company objectives are set in purely financial terms – earnings per share, return on capital employed, and so on – subsequent marketing analysis may show that some of these are unobtainable, and that they should be modified.

When objectives are agreed, then strategy becomes the means of achieving them.

■ Marketing strategy is the broad, long-term description of how the company will compete in its chosen markets and segments.

The strategy will guide the shorter-term tactics, which will need to be adapted to the constant changes in circumstances which are inevitable over the years; the strategy will keep the company moving towards its goal rather than allowing it to be blown about rudderless.

Types of strategy

The interaction between marketing and business strategy is shown by the way we think of types of strategy. One of the best-known suggests that there are only four basic or generic competitive strategies, as shown in Figure 10.1 (Porter 1990). This says that to succeed, a firm must choose whether to compete on a broad front or to attack narrower targets; and that within each it must choose either cost leadership or differentiation. Anything else risks being 'stuck in the middle', vulnerable to competitors who either have lower costs, or are better than you at differentiating themselves in the eyes of buyers.

Thus in shipbuilding, Japanese yards offer a wide range of ships

Figure 10.1 Porter's generic strategies

Competitive advantage

Lower cost   Differentiation

		Lower cost	Differentiation
	Broad target	1 Cost leadership	2 Differentiation
Competitive scope			
	Narrow target	3A Cost focus	3B Differentiation focus

of very high quality at premium prices (differentiation); Koreans offer good but not premium quality at lower prices (cost leadership); some Scandinavian firms offer specialised ships of high quality and price (focused differentiation); and some Chinese yards offer a narrow range of simple ships at low prices (cost focus).

These are both general business and marketing strategies. Marketing, in its analysis of where markets are going and how the firm can best compete, must influence the firm's choice, though obviously there are other considerations such as the technology base and finance available.

Another typology is more directly marketing oriented; it is known as the Ansoff matrix, and is shown in Figure 10.2. As most plans are looking for growth, then unless your existing products are going to go on growing in your existing markets (possible but unlikely), you are going to need to find growth elsewhere. In the nature of things, if your board sees growth from existing products, they will almost certainly ask for further growth on top of that.

The Ansoff matrix shows that we can look for growth from

Figure 10.2 Ansoff's matrix

	Markets	
	Existing	New
Existing	Market penetration	Market development
Products		
New	Product development	Diversification

products we know and markets we are familiar with; and also from new products and markets. The point of the matrix is not only to help us to structure our thinking about where to find extra sales, but also to draw attention to the fact that there are different levels of risk attached to the different strategies. Normally, we expect that the lowest levels of risk are associated with things we know well – our existing products and markets. The further we move away from these, in either direction, the greater the risk. The riskiest strategy is diversification, when we launch new products into new markets. Which strategy we choose will therefore depend on how much growth we want, how much is available from the safest expansion methods, and what our attitude to risk is.

Other ways of classifying strategies are rather broad, such as mass market against niche; or premium quality/price against cheap and cheerful. One split which is found in consumer marketing may need explanation: push and pull strategies.

■ *A pull strategy* is one in which the manufacturer has strong brands which are supported by heavy advertising. The strategy is to create consumer demand which will 'pull' the brand through the distribution channels.

■ *A push strategy*, on the other hand, uses trade terms and promotions, perhaps with heavy selling emphasis, to load the distribution channels with the products. It is then assumed that the distributors will 'push' the products out on to the market.

Try to apply these classifications to your firm's strategy or strategies, using Worksheet 10.1.

Identifying and evaluating your strategy

We have said that a strategy must have objectives, and a set of rules for competing in our chosen markets. An example of this in a marketing strategy would be:

■ *Objective*: to be number one or two brand in our (defined) consumer markets.
■ *Strategy*: each brand must have a functional point of difference from competitors and be better quality as perceived by consumers; each will be supported by heavy advertising (at least equal weight to competitors), and little trade promotion; a price premium of 5 per cent over the nearest rival will be sought.

This is rather general, but at least it would provide guidance as to what specific marketing actions were and were not acceptable. It would also guide resource allocation decisions, and help with difficult product policy decisions such as which products to drop and which to invest in.

Does your company have a defined marketing strategy? Write down in Worksheet 10.2 in one or more sentences what that strategy is.

At the very beginning of this book we said that marketing was about matching – matching what the company offers to customers, consumers and competitors. The marketing strategy must therefore pass this test. It must start from where the company is and what it can and cannot do. It must meet the needs of buyers, both final buyers and intermediaries. It must differentiate the company's offering from competitors.

The later section on planning will include some specific checks, but in the meantime try evaluating your existing strategy (or the

WORKSHEET 10.1 CLASSIFYING STRATEGIES

■ How does your firm compete in its chosen markets?
Does it have a generic strategy, or a number of different
strategies? Tick those strategies you think your firm is
following; if there is more than one, note this (e.g.
Product A against Cost leadership, Product B against
Cost focus etc.). Does a coherent picture emerge?

Strategic type

1 Porter's generic strategies:
   Cost leadership
   Differentiation
   Cost focus
   Focused differentiation

2 Ansoff's matrix:
   Market penetration
   Market development
   Product development
   Diversification

3 Mass market

4 Niche

5 Premium

6 Value for money

7 Cheap

8 Offensive

9 Defensive

10 Push

11 Pull

Conclusions

WORKSHEET 10.2 DEFINING STRATEGY

■ Write down in one or more sentences what your firm's strategy is, either overall or for a particular product/ market. Use concepts from the book such as the four Ps, positioning and segmentation if they are helpful.

Strategy for ....

We will compete in ....
(target market/s by) ....

---

one you are developing as you work through this chapter) against the list of questions in Worksheet 10.3. You may not be able to answer all the questions, but they will perhaps direct your thinking about what strategy means.

A strategy, if it is to mean anything, must be the result of careful thought and analysis. It is a long-term commitment, and cannot be changed frequently. It needs to be sold within the company, and accepted so that whatever resources are needed for its implementation are committed. To do that, it must obviously offer a good chance of delivering, that is of meeting the company's overall

WORKSHEET 10.3 EVALUATING STRATEGIES

■ Evaluate your current strategy as described in Worksheet 10.2, using the following criteria. Most require a qualitative rating, so no conclusion may be reached as to whether the strategy is 'good' or 'bad'; but you should identify areas of possible weakness or actions which need to be taken.

Cost

1 How will this be financed?

2 How different is it from previous strategies?

3 For the strategy to succeed, what changes in behaviour are necessary?

Channels   *Buyers/users*

4 What are the barriers to those?

5 What does the strategy do to encourage the changes and avoid the barriers?

6 What are the critical success factors for this strategy? Tick those you control

7 What assumptions were made under each heading about the strategy, and how certain are you of each?

                          Assumption   *How certain*

Environment
Market
Customers
Consumers
Competitors

8 What will happen if the assumptions are wrong?

9 What skills are needed to implement the strategy?

Skills   *Rating*

10 Rate the firm on the level of each skill you have at present (1–10)

11 How well does the strategy fit the company?

12 Is it tightly targeted at the chosen market segment?

13 How different is it from competitors?

objectives; it must also fit the company's resource base, skills and culture (or if it does not, it should include ways of getting from where you are to where you need to be).

Finding a good strategy is also a matter of flair and creativity – of jumping a gap, putting together ideas in a way no-one else has done, finding a way of doing things that no competitor has thought of. There are creativity techniques to help in this (brainstorming, for example), and if a shortage of good ideas is a problem in your organisation it may be worth trying some. It is certainly worth trying very hard to think up alternative strategies. Often these turn out to be impracticable in some way; but the real breakthroughs are made by those who do something different.

DEVELOPING A MARKETING PLAN

Planning, like strategy, has received something of a bad name in some firms, mainly by being over-sold. When it has been imposed from the top down, without careful preparation, it has often been resented. Line managers in particular have found it bureaucratic, intrusive and unhelpful. The volatility of many markets in recent years has helped to confirm some people in their view that planning is a waste of time and effort.

That is a pity, for it is obvious that *some* planning is needed. Depending on the type of firm, we need to know: how many products to manufacture, and therefore what components and supplies to buy; how many personnel of what type we will need; what to say to which customers about what we are offering – and so on. Most of these relate back, directly or indirectly, to the market and to our expected sales.

All firms are planning – to a greater or lesser extent – because they have to. They may not call it planning, and much of it is done implicitly and informally. What this chapter argues is that the the process will be better if it is made more explicit, and probably a little more formal – though definitely not bureaucratic.

Basically, good planning delivers two sorts of benefit: being prepared, and communication and co-ordination.

■ *Being prepared* implies that the firm will be ready to take advantage of opportunities and to meet threats, both expected and unexpected; it will take profitable opportunities as they arise, and not waste too much effort chasing mirages.
■ *Communication and co-ordination* refers to the need for communication between departments and individuals without which

efficient and effective co-ordination of the firm's efforts is impossible.

Although both seem simple and straightforward, most managers will recognise that they do not occur naturally; indeed their counterparts (lack of preparedness, absence of communication, faulty co-ordination) are at the root of many problems.

Marketing planning, as we have said, is part of the overall company planning effort. Where a planning system does not exist, it takes time to introduce successfully. It must be carefully fitted to the size and nature of the firm, increasing in complexity only reluctantly and because of the increasing size and complexity of the company, its products and its markets.

It should encourage line managers to take responsibility for the process, and to exercise their creativity. The need for co-ordination and control (and there certainly is such a need) must be balanced against the need to motivate line managers and to encourage their radical thinking.

To succeed, a marketing planning process should have the following characteristics:

- Have active top management involvement
- Be integrated into the overall business planning system
- Be iterative, with feedback from lower levels to higher
- Have explored the possible impact of changes elsewhere in the firm (technology, finance, personnel) on marketing programmes, and vice versa
- Be based on a deep understanding of the forces driving its markets
- Have looked at possible changes in these forces
- Have examined the likely actions of existing and potential new competitors
- Have checked the feasibility of its planned programmes against the firm's resources as well as external factors such as channels and buyers

If you have a marketing planning system, check it against these criteria. If you do not have one, you may like to use them as a basis for questions to ask about marketing plans that are presented – or as a basis for building a new planning system.

Stages in marketing planning

In any planning system, from the most informal annual budgeting to the most complex and formal corporate planning, there is a cycle. This is usually annual, as firms work on an annual basis for their accounting, and there are often annual rhythms in the market too.

Generally speaking, the more complicated the firm and therefore its planning (because of the need for more co-ordination between functions, levels and business units), the longer the planning cycle will be. Thus in a fairly complicated company, planning for next year may start nine months or more earlier, with review and consolidation stages leading up to agreement of the complete plan some three months before the start of the year.

In fact, of course, the planning cycle is going on all the time, since managers are reviewing progress this year against targets while looking forward to next year. What is happening now will feed forward into the objectives and plans for the future.

The other consideration is that most firms need to plan more than one year ahead. As markets have become more volatile and difficult to predict, some people have argued that any long-term planning is useless. In some markets they may be right, as long as you can plan the sort of flexibility in your operations which will allow you to respond to whatever happens. Most firms, however, have lead times which they need in order to develop towards their goals. These lead times may reflect the time it takes to commission and build a new production plant; in marketing terms, it may be a case of how long it takes to develop and launch a range of new products, or to reach a certain position in the market. If it will take five years to reach a certain position (for example to be the preferred choice amongst business travellers on certain airline routes), the intermediate steps must be planned for.

■ Every one-year plan, therefore, must be set in the context of longer-term plans, and should contain the intermediate goals leading towards the five-year (or whatever period is relevant) goals.

The stages which form the planning cycle are, in full:

■ Corporate objectives

■ Situation analysis
  – environmental scan
  – marketing audit
      internal
      markets
      customers
      consumers
      competitors
  – key SWOT
■ Assumptions made about future changes in driving forces
  – environmental
  – markets
  – customers
  – consumers
  – competitors
■ Definition of critical success factors
■ Marketing objectives – long term and next year
■ Generation of alternative strategies
■ Evaluation of strategies against objectives, situation analysis and assumptions
■ Choice of strategy/ies
■ Outline plan for five years
■ Detailed planning for next year
  – marketing mix for each segment
  – costing
■ Identification of possible blockages
■ Contingency plans
■ Design of measurement and control system
■ Presentation and agreement of final plan
■ Implementation and review.

This looks complicated and exhausting. In fact, most of the work has already been done in the worksheets in the earlier chapters of this book; if you have worked your way through those, you have the basis of a marketing plan. Not all firms may need to go in detail through absolutely every stage: a small, simple firm may be able to compress stages or skip. But it is worth at least thinking through each one to see what effect it might have on your final plan.

One element which has not been mentioned so far is blockages. Any manager knows that 'The best-laid schemes o' mice and men gang aft a-gley.' There will always be unexpected snags which crop up; but there may also be problems which can to some extent be foreseen. If a blockage is something we may be able to do something about, it makes sense to try to do so; if there is nothing we can do, we should resign ourselves to the inevitable – but it still makes sense to know in advance that it may happen. Use Worksheet 10.4 to identify possible blockages and action to circumvent them.

The whole point of the planning system is to answer three apparently simple but in fact searching questions:

- Where are we now?
- Where do we want to go?
- How do we get there?

The planning system you adopt should suit your company's particular circumstances, and should enable you to find answers to those questions.

WORKSHEET 10.4 BLOCKAGES

- Identify the blockages which may prevent the achievement of the objectives. These may be internal (politics, finance, organisation structure ...) or external (market changes, competitive actions ...). Against each, think of one or more actions which could be taken to prevent or avoid the blockage.

  Blockages   *Actions*

  Internal

  External

Contents of the plan

It follows that the precise form and content of the marketing plan will vary according to the size and nature of the firm. It need not (indeed, should not) contain all the detailed facts, figures and arguments which have gone into each stage. The person developing and presenting the plan should have all those in reserve to back up the argument, but they do not need to be printed in full in a giant report. As plans progress up through the levels of the organisation, they will be consolidated and summarised. What is important is that the *thinking* behind the plan has been carried out thoroughly at each stage, not the final format of the plan.

As a minimum, a marketing plan should have the following headings:

1   Situation analysis, including year-to-date results against plan, and diagnosis
2   Objectives: next year, five years (or whatever period is chosen)
3   Assumptions
4   Strategies (brief description)
5   Detailed plan for each element of the mix, including timing
6   Projected sales by period
7   Costs
8   Control measures.

The key parts are the detailed plans in sections 4–7; in many companies the marketing plan for each brand may concentrate on those, and be summarised in a page or two of numbers. This is fine, *as long as the strategic thinking has been done.*

For example, you used Worksheet 10.3 to test a strategy. Now use Worksheet 10.5 to further test the quality of the planning. This checks the strategy adopted against diagnoses made earlier about the environmental factors which you identified and against your view of the firm's Strengths, Weaknesses, Opportunities and Threats. It is surprisingly easy to go through each stage, and then forget the earlier work when you come to put the plan together.

IMPLEMENTATION AND CONTROL

Many writers in recent years have argued that strategy and planning are not the problems: it is poor implementation that lets

WORKSHEET 10.5 STRATEGIC FIT

■ Take your current strategy described earlier, and an
alternative strategy which you would like to consider,
and see how they fit with the diagnoses you made about
environmental factors which will affect you and your
SWOT analysis. Put a plus sign if the factor will help the
strategy and a minus sign if it will work against it. To be
more sophisticated, you may wish to weight the factors
by relative importance.

	Current strategy	*Alternative strategy*
Environmental factors		
Political/legal		
Economic		
Social/cultural		
Technological		
Other		
Strengths		
Weaknesses		
Opportunities		
Threats		
Total score		

firms down. Most managers will know of occasions when their firm has made mistakes which were not about grand strategy, but simply about doing the right things at the right time. Much of this is a question of basic management skills, and regretfully there are also internal blockages caused by politics; but there are also three areas in marketing planning and implementation which bear particular concentration, as they seem to be associated with successful firms when they are well managed, and conversely with failure when they are poorly managed. The three areas are:

- understanding the customer/consumer
- differentiation of the product and mix
- teamwork

In a sense, this whole book has been about the first two. A deep understanding of the customer and consumer is the theme which runs throughout, and stress has been laid constantly on the absolute need to understand the role of the product-in-use in buyers' and users' lives. Without that, no planning, however sophisticated, will be of any use.

Differentiation of your offering from competitors has also been stressed throughout. The most common failures are of 'me-too' products and marketing plans which offer nothing different from what is already available. Finding and sustaining a real point of difference based on an understanding of buyers' needs is a tremendous challenge – but it must remain the heart of what marketing can do for the firm.

If it could be argued that these two are more concerned with the planning phase than implementation, the answer is that too often issues of implementation seem to over-ride the thinking that has gone before. What is easy, or what we have always done, or what we can afford become the criteria, especially in a crisis. This must be resisted.

Teamwork, however, is central to success in planning and most particularly in implementation. We have talked of the need for communication and co-ordination. If departments do not talk to each other and co-ordinate their actions, no plan can succeed. Now more than ever before, the efforts of the firm as a whole need to be geared up to provide quality products and service. There is simply no excuse for squabbling and turf disputes which get in the

WORKSHEET 10.6 COMMUNICATION AND CO-ORDINATION

> ■ Which departments need to communicate with each
> other, and whose activities need to be co-ordinated in
> order for the marketing plan to succeed? List the main
> elements of the plan, (e.g. launch new product, improve
> customer service ...) and against each tick which func-
> tions ought to be working together; then comment on
> how well this is done at present.
>
> *Departments/functions*
>
> *Marketing   Sales   Production   R&D   Accounts   Rating*
>
> *Elements*
> *of plan*

way of delivering what customers want. Unfortunately, these
problems do exist in many firms; it is the responsibility of senior
management to make sure that they are identified and minimised.
Marketing cannot work on its own, but only as part of a team
involving all the major functions.

Use Worksheet 10.6 to identify which departments need to
communicate and be co-ordinated for the marketing plan to
succeed; comment on how well this is happening at the moment.

Finally, think about control measures. A plan which has no
feedback is out of control, since small (and sometimes major)
adjustments need to be made as you go through the year. Unless
you know what is happening, you are not in charge. The work in
Chapter 4 on marketing information will have given you some
ideas, but now you need to think specifically about the marketing
plan. Ideally you should monitor progress towards each objective.
With major objectives such as sales this may be straightforward
(though you may need to think about how sales should be analysed

WORKSHEET 10.7 FEEDBACK MEASURES

> ■ For each marketing objective in your plan, identify what
> feedback measure will allow you to monitor progress
> towards it, and the source of the feedback. Then say who
> should receive each item of feedback, and how often. Set
> control limits on variations which are acceptable (e.g.
> plus or minus 10 per cent), and specify what action
> should be taken if the measure falls outside those limits.

Objective	Feedback measure and source	Who should receive	Frequency	Variation allowed	Action

and reported); with other objectives such as improving customer
service, more thought and new measures may be needed. Use
Worksheet 10.7 to design a control system.

At this stage, we have worked our way through the book. You
should now have a basic understanding of what marketing is about,
and how you can apply it in your organisation (whether you make
physical products, offer commercial services, or indeed work in a
not-for-profit institution). Marketing is complex to apply in practice, but challenging and fascinating. Good luck!

References

Drucker, P. (1967) *Managing for Results*, London: Pan Books.

Kotler, P. (1991) *Marketing Management*, 7th edition, Englewood Cliffs, NJ: Prentice-Hall.

Piercy, N. (1992) *Market-Led Strategic Growth*, Oxford: Butterworth-Heinemann.

Porter, M. (1990) *The Competitive Advantage of Nations*, New York: Free Press.

Randall, G. (1990) *Marketing to the Retail Trade*, London: Heinemann.

Randall, G. (1993) *Principles of Marketing*, London: Routledge.

Randall, G. (1994) *Trade Marketing Strategies*, London: Heinemann.

Winkler, J. (1983) *Pricing for Results*, London: Heinemann.